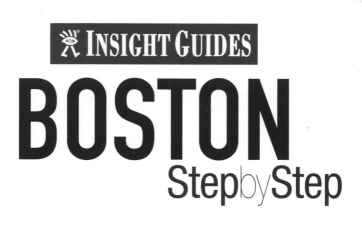

INSIGHT GUIDES

BOSTON
StepbyStep

Discovery
CHANNEL

APA PUBLICATIONS L
Part of the Langenscheidt Publishing Group

CONTENTS

ABOUT THIS BOOK

This *Step by Step Guide* has been produced by the editors of Insight Guides, whose books have set the standard for visual travel guides since 1970. With top-quality photography and authoritative recommendations, this guidebook brings you the very best of Boston in a series of 16 tailor-made tours.

WALKS AND TOURS

The tours in the book provide something to suit all budgets, tastes, and trip lengths. As well as covering Boston's many classic attractions, the routes track lesser-known sights and up-and-coming areas; there are also excursions for those who want to extend their visit outside the city.

The tours embrace a range of interests, so whether you are a history buff, an art-lover, a gourmet, a shopaholic, or have kids to entertain, you will find an option to suit.

We recommend that you read the whole of a tour before setting out. This should help you to familiarize yourself with the route and enable you to plan where to stop for refreshments –

Above: skyline view and Charles River; statue of Paul Revere in the North End; Christian Science Plaza at night; baseball at Fenway Park, home of the Red Sox; lobster weathervane at the Waterfront.

options for this are shown in the 'Food and Drink' boxes, recognizable by the knife and fork sign, on most pages.

For our pick of the walks by theme, consult Recommended Tours For… *(see pp.6–7).*

OVERVIEW

The tours are set in context by this introductory section, giving an overview of the city to set the scene, plus background information on food and drink, shopping, sports and entertainment. A succinct history timeline highlights the key events that have shaped Boston over the centuries.

DIRECTORY

Also supporting the tours is a Directory chapter, comprising a user-friendly, clearly organized A–Z of practical information, our pick of where to stay while you are in the city, select restaurant listings (complementing the more low-key cafés and restaurants that feature within the tours themselves), and recommended nightlife venues.

The Author

During his career as a journalist and photographer, award-winning travel writer Simon Richmond has lived in several cities, including London, Tokyo, and Sydney. He has authored and contributed to over 30 different travel guidebooks from Cape Town to the Trans-Siberian Railway, as well as restaurant and activity guides. His home for the last three years has been Boston, which he has explored thoroughly with his partner Tonny, who has lived there for over two decades. Compact, historic, but also modern, Boston is, in Simon's view, one of the best cities in the world for discovering on foot.

This book builds on previous work by travel writer Marcus Brooke, who used to teach at Harvard and MIT.

Margin Tips
Shopping tips, historical facts, handy hints and information on activities help visitors make the most of their time in Boston.

Feature Boxes
Notable topics are highlighted in these special boxes.

Key Facts Box
This box gives details of the distance covered on the tour, plus an estimate of how long it should take. It also states where the route starts and finishes, and gives key travel information such as which days are best to do the route or handy transport tips.

Route Map
Detailed cartography shows the tour clearly plotted with numbered dots. For more detailed mapping, see the pull-out map slotted inside the back cover.

Food and Drink
Recommendations of where to stop for refreshment are given in these boxes. The numbers prior to each restaurant/café name link to references in the main text. On city maps, restaurants are plotted.

The $ signs at the end of each entry reflect the approximate cost of a three-course dinner for one, excluding beverages, tax, and tip. These should be seen as a guide only. Price ranges, also quoted on the inside back flap for easy reference, are as follows:

$$$$ $60 and above
$$$ $40–60
$$ $20–40
$ $20 and below

Footers
Those on the left-hand page give the tour name plus, where relevant, a map reference; those on the right-hand page show the main attraction on the double page.

ESCAPING THE CROWDS

Head to the Charles River (walk 4) or to the Back Bay Fens (walk 7) for green spaces. Alternatively, the tranquil residential streets of Beacon Hill (walk 5) are generally crowd-free. For the ultimate escape, take a ferry to one of the Harbor Islands (tour 11).

RECOMMENDED TOURS FOR...

CHILDREN

The Aquarium and the Children's Museum (walk 10) will be hits with the little ones, as will the Museum of Science (walk 4). The USS *Constitution* in Charlestown (walk 2) and the Plimoth Plantation in Plymouth (tour 15) are both educational and fun.

SCIENCE & TECHNOLOGY

The Museum of Science and the MIT Museum and campus (walk 4) have outstanding boffin appeal, as do Harvard's Peabody Museum and Museum of Natural History (walk 3).

WATERSIDE VIEWS

You are seldom far from water in Boston, be it the Charles River (walk 4) or Boston Harbor (walks 2 and 10). To get out on the water, take a ferry to the Harbor Islands (tour 11) or Provincetown, Cape Cod (tour 16).

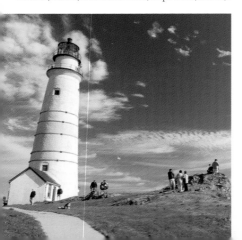

REVOLUTIONARY BOSTON

Follow the Freedom Trail of revolutionary sites through Boston's Downtown (walk 1), North End and Charlestown (walk 2), then head out of town to follow the 'Battle Road' between Lexington and Concord (tour 14).

ART ENTHUSIASTS

If you love art, don't miss the Museum of Fine Arts and Isabella Stewart Gardner Museum (walk 8), or the Institute of Contemporary Art (walk 10). Salem's Peabody Essex Museum (tour 12), Cape Ann's art colonies (tour 13), and Provincetown's galleries (tour 16) are also worthwhile.

ARCHITECTURE

Beacon Hill (walk 5), Back Bay (walk 6), and the South End (walk 9) are all packed with grand Bostonian architecture from the 17th through early 20th centuries. MIT's Stata Center (walk 4) and the Institute of Contemporary Art at Fort Point (walk 10) are fantastic 21st-century additions to the city.

FOOD AND WINE

Dine out in either the North End (walk 2) or South End (walk 9), and your stomach will be very happy. Harvard Square (walk 3) is also a fine place to chow down, as is Newbury Street in Back Bay (walk 6).

SHOPPERS

Check out Charles Street's antiques shops (walk 5), Newbury Street's boutiques (walk 6), Harvard's bookstores (walk 3), and the South End's quirky independent stores (walk 9).

PARKS AND GARDENS

Boston's Emerald Necklace of parks and gardens extends from the Common (walk 1) through the Public Garden (walk 5) and Commonwealth Avenue's central boulevard (walk 6) to the Back Bay Fens (walk 7). The Charles River Esplanade (walk 4) is also a strolling pleasure.

OVERVIEW

An overview of Boston's geography, character, and culture, plus illuminating background information on food and drink, shopping, sports, entertainment, and history.

CITY INTRODUCTION

Both traditional and modern, Boston is considered the most 'European' of American cities – hardly surprising given its British colonial roots. But this is also the birthplace of the country's independence, and home to some of its most illustrious Ivy League institutions.

Emerald Necklace
The Emerald Necklace – a corridor of interlinked parklands and gardens stretching for 7 miles (11km) from Boston Common to Franklin Park – was designed by Frederick Law Olmsted (1822–1903). He also conceived the beautiful Esplanade park that hugs the south bank of the Charles River, but which was not built until the 1930s, and New York's Central Park.

Historic Landmarks
The US National Parks Service records 183 National Historic Landmarks in the state of Massachusetts; only New York state beats it with 257. A good proportion of these sites are found in the Boston city area and surrounding towns such as Concord, Lexington, Plymouth, Provincetown, and Salem.

Boston is small (population 590,000) and compact (48 sq. miles/124 sq. km), making it an ideal city for discovering on foot. By size it may only be the 20th-largest city in the US, but in terms of its historical legacy Boston is huge. Among the lofty phrases coined to describe the city are the 'Cradle of Liberty', the 'Athens of America', and 'the Hub of the Universe' (a variant of the latter was first used by one of Boston's greatest literary sons Oliver Wendell Holmes to describe the State House).

A Rich Heritage

Many visitors come here to walk in the footsteps of the Founding Fathers and soak up the Old World atmosphere that nurtured some of America's most gifted artistic, mercantile, and political talents, including the poet Henry Wadsworth Longfellow (1807–82), the artist John Singer Sargent (1856–1925), and President John F. Kennedy (1917–63). Boston plays up to this rich heritage in projects such as the Freedom Trail *(see p.25)*, the Black Heritage Trail *(see feature, p.53)*, and the Battle Road Trail *(see p.85)* between Lexington and Concord. That many historical monuments and sites have been preserved as part of the fabric of the city is a large part of Boston's appeal.

HARBOR CITY

Boston's fortunes first came from its harbor, and this was a pivotal part of the city up until the early 20th century. With the end of the Big Dig *(see feature, p.13)* and the city's promotion of the HarborWalk route *(see p.75)*, attention is now flowing back to the long-neglected seashore. From May to mid-October you can take public ferries out to some of the 34 islands that are one of the city's biggest, yet least-known, natural assets *(see p.76)*. Another is its Emerald Necklace of parks and gardens *(see margin, left)* – Boston is one of America's greenest cities.

TWO CITIES IN ONE

The graceful Charles River splits Boston to the south from the separate city of Cambridge, home to the Ivy League institutions Harvard and MIT, to the north. For all practical purposes the two cities interact as one, and Boston's efficient, clean, and safe subway system (known simply as the 'T') makes shuttling between the two sides a breeze. Walkers and cyclists can also make use of dedicated paths traversing eight bridges between Harvard and the river's mouth into the harbor.

SEAT OF LEARNING

Spreading out from this central neighborhood is Greater Boston, which consists of nearly 100 towns with a total population of about 3 million. A not insignificant portion of that number is made up of young people who flock to the area's multiple seats of higher education, of which Harvard and MIT are but the cream of the crop. Boston University alone – its campus dominating the area around Commonwealth Avenue west of Kenmore Square – has 30,000 students enrolled. All this adds up to a liberal and vibrant atmosphere for a city that respects its past, but also has one foot striding into the future.

ETHNIC DIVERSITY

The Boston area has long been a magnet for immigrants. The community most associated with the city are the Irish: they currently make up about 16 per cent of the population and remain the largest ethnic group, with a strong cultural influence in areas such as Jamaica Plain and South Boston. The Italian community, most visible in the North End (see p.32), has given the city its current mayor, Thomas Menino – a popular politician and the first non-Irish mayor since 1884. Rounding out the city's ethnic diversity are more recent immigrants from Brazil, Vietnam, and China.

Boston Brahmins
For all this multiculturalism, Boston remains best-known for its Brahmins – the blue-blooded stock who can trace their ancestry back to the original 17th-century inhabitants of Massachusetts Bay Colony. Thanks to the philanthropic inclinations of many old Bostonian families, the city can share with one and all a treasure trove of art and culture, such as that on display at the wonderful Museum of Fine Arts (see p.64). If this is what you are interested in, then a trip to nearby Salem (see p.78) to view the equally impressive collections of the Peabody Essex Museum is also recommended.

Above from far left: playing chess in Harvard Square; Boston skyline; canine Red Sox fan.

Below: students outside Harvard's Biological Laboratories.

Above from left:
the Christian Science
Plaza was designed
by I.M. Pei; Public
Garden in fall; Old
State House.

ARCHITECTURAL DEVELOPMENT

What comes to mind when most people think of Boston's architecture are red-brick terrace houses and the golden dome of the State House. People used to the strict grid plan of other American cities are also wrong-footed by the meandering roads of its more historical areas, such as Downtown, the North End, and Charlestown. However, over the four centuries since it was settled, much has changed in Boston's built landscape, and, like any dynamic city, it is still evolving.

The Colonial Era

Not much from the earliest colonial period is left in Boston, mainly because the predominantly wooden houses of those days fell victim to frequent fires. Even as late as 1872 Boston was suffering catastrophic blazes: the Great Fire of that year wiped out most of the city center. The sole wooden construction from the 17th century that remains in central Boston is the Paul Revere House *(see p.33)* built in 1680. The city burghers learned their lesson from these conflagrations and ditched wood in favor of brick and stone. Note the contrast between the Tudor-style Revere House and its brick-built neighbor the Pierce-Hichborn House from 1711, a classic example of Georgian architecture along with the Old State House *(see p.29)*, dating from 1713.

The 18th and 19th Centuries

The architect most associated with Boston is Charles Bulfinch (1763–1844). The scion of a wealthy family, he traveled Europe soaking up ideas and influences that he later translated into the designs of friends' houses in Beacon Hill *(see pp.51, 52, and 55)*. The success of the homes led to Bulfinch being commissioned to design the new State House *(see p.51)* in 1798, which was something of a dry run for his US Capitol Building in Washington, DC.

By the early decades of the 19th century, land-reclamation projects were changing the shape of the city. Where the handsome terraces and garden squares of the South End *(see p.68)* and the grand mansions and boulevards of Back Bay *(see p.56)* now stand was once sea water and swamp. Boston's accumu-

Below: State House.

lated wealth and culture is reflected in the elaborate buildings from this era, such as the Ames-Webster Mansion, built in 1872, and the even more flamboyant Burrage House (1889).

Italian Renaissance, neo-Gothic, and neo-Romanesque styles were all the rage. You can spot all these motifs around Copley Square, which is crowned by the Boston Public Library *(see p.59)*, designed by Charles McKim (1847–1909) and one of the city's most impressive public buildings. Facing the library is Trinity Church, a masterpiece by Henry Hobson Richardson (1838–86), another great American architect.

The 20th Century

Boston got its first skyscraper in 1915, but high-rise buildings never really caught on here. The Prudential Tower (1965) and John Hancock Tower (1975) stand out mainly because there are so few other skyscrapers in the city. Boston's style of contemporary inner-city regeneration has, instead, been on a more human scale. First came the demolition of the old West End and construction of Government Center – a not entirely harmonious project that is softened by the success of the nearby Faneuil Hall-Quincy Market complex. Rising real-estate prices helped revive Back Bay and later the South End, both of which fell into decline in the middle of the 20th century.

The 21st Century

The completion of the massive engineering project known as the Big Dig *(see feature, below)* has reconnected the city with the harbor, enabling the focus to shift to the South Boston Seaport district. Here you will find the new Institute of Contemporary Art *(see p.75)*, which, along with the Frank Gehry-designed Stata Center *(see p.48)* over in the Massachusetts Institute of Technology (MIT), is a modern-day example of the cutting-edge architecture that Boston has dabbled in right through its history. Also shaping up for a facelift is the Downtown area, with a new residential and business tower rising on the site of the old Filene's Basement, a much-loved discount store that promises to return once all the construction is over *(see margin, p.17)*.

Boston Lingo

Native Bostonians have a distinctive way of talking. The accent tends to result in an elongated 'a' and elided 'r' – hence 'Hahvahd Yahd', rather than Harvard Yard. Once you have got used to that, memorize the following commonly used shorthand to some of the city's locations: Com Ave – Commonwealth Avenue; JP – Jamaica Plain; Mass Ave – Massachusetts Avenue; Mem Drive – Memorial Drive; The Pike – The Massachusetts Turnpike.

The End of the Big Dig

The project to bury the Central Artery – the raised highway that sliced the harbor off from the Downtown area – in a tunnel beneath the city was known as the Big Dig. It took over a decade to complete, causing massive disruption, and cost in excess of $15 billion, making it one of the most expensive and controversial American civil engineering projects of recent times. The results, though, have widely been welcomed. Traffic flows much more freely across the city now, and the harbor and previously cut-off neighborhoods such as the North End are directly accessible via a pleasant strip of parkland known as the Rose Kennedy Greenway. The highway emerges from its tunnel to cross the spectacular Leonard P. Zakim Bridge (pictured), named after a local civil-rights activist.

FOOD AND DRINK

Once famous for its baked beans and meat-and-two-veg dinners, Boston cuisine today is equal parts traditional and contemporary. Beer is taken seriously, but there are also cool cocktail bars and hip cafés in which to relax.

Why Beantown?
Back in the 18th century Boston was awash with molasses shipped in from the Caribbean as part of the rum trade. These were mixed with salt pork and beans to make baked beans, once the quint- essential Boston dish – hence the nickname Beantown. These days baked beans are not a common menu item; if you fancy trying them, Union Oyster House *(see p.31)* and Durgin Park *(see p.73)* both serve the dish.

LOCAL SPECIALTIES

New England cooking is all about traditional American produce, such as cranberries, corn, and seafood. Local specialties include creamy clam chow- der, scrod (small, tender haddock or cod) and steamers (clams with broth and butter). Be sure to sample at least one lobster roll – a soft-bread roll sandwich stuffed with lobster meat typically mixed with mayonnaise.

As you would expect for somewhere on the coast, you will find plenty of this style of cuisine in Boston itself, much of it excellent.

HUMBLE TO HIGH-CLASS

Some of the city's best dining experi- ences are in the humblest of joints, be it enjoying a hearty breakfast or sand- wich at Charlie's Sandwich Shoppe *(see p.68)* or simply delicious fish and chips at The Daily Catch *(see p.33)*. That said, Boston also has a well-deserved reputation for contemporary American dining, as practiced by celebrity chefs such as Ken Oringer, of Clio and La Verdad Taqueria *(see pp.111 and 62)*, Todd English of Figs and Olives *(see pp.39 and 115)*, and Barbara Lynch of No. 9 Park *(see p.117)*.

Right: Hood (a home- grown dairy business) Milk Bottle; beer and burger.

ETHNIC AND TRENDY

Boston's diverse immigrant population has also bequeathed it a fine range of ethnic restaurants.

Chinatown is primarily packed with – you guessed it – Chinese restaurants, but it also has a smattering of Malaysian, Vietnamese, and Japanese eateries too.

The North End's vibe is almost exclusively Italian – from simple red-and-white-tablecloth cafés to sleek temples to regional *cucine*. For the trendiest dining spots, the South End and its SoWa (South of Washington) district are the places to head – between Tremont Street and Washington Avenue you will never go hungry.

Seafood, naturally, is a big feature of the Waterfront and up-and-coming Fort Point Channel areas, while the academic areas around Harvard and MIT are prime hunting grounds for good-value, atmospherically vibrant, and cosmopolitan restaurants and cafés. Cambridge's reputation for healthy organic cooking is deserved, but the town is also no slouch at fine dining. When it comes to discovering hot new chefs, it is this side of the Charles River that often proves the more fertile.

BARS

The immigrant community most associated with Boston is that from Ireland. It should come as no surprise then that Irish bars seem to be located on every other corner of the city. A few are authentic, and worth visiting for a pint or two *(see pp.120–2 for recommendations)*; others are kitsch tourist traps and best avoided.

Hip cocktail bars are also catching on, but Boston is too small a town to generate the kind of happening scene you would find in New York or London.

CAFÉS

It is hard to beat the North End's collection of cafés for an espresso or cappuccino that hits the spot. Also, do not pass up the chance of hanging with students in the cafés of Harvard Square. Both here and on Newbury Street in Back Bay tea-lovers will be heartened to know that the city's reputation for dumping the leaf in the harbor has been overturned at Tealuxe (0 Brattle Street and 108 Newbury Street).

Above from far left: freshly cooked lobster; Union Oyster House.

Reservations
Boston is not New York, so scoring a table at even the hottest places is well within the reach of ordinary mortals. Nevertheless, you would be well advised to make an advance booking for Friday or Saturday nights: try the online booking service www.open table.com. Note that some places do not take reservations at all, so turn up early or be prepared to wait.

Beer City

Founding father Samuel Adams was a brewmaster, so it is natural that one of the city's principal breweries should have adopted his name. Having started out as a micro-brewery in 1985, Sam Adams now produces a fine range of ales found in bars across the city. Micro-breweries that have stayed micro include Boston Beer Works, with branches near Fenway Park and the North End, Cambridge Brewing Company near MIT, and John Harvard's Brew House near Harvard Square. Back Bay's Bukowski Tavern (50 Dalton Street; tel: 617-437-9999) stocks over 100 different brews.

SHOPPING

Boston's shopping does not stop at Red Sox souvenirs or a sweatshirt from Harvard or MIT. While tourists flock to the retail hubs of Faneuil Hall-Quincy Market and Newbury Street, do not miss the variety of shops that are tucked away in the South End and the side streets of Harvard.

Opening Times

Most stores open Mon–Sat 9am–7pm, and shopping malls generally stay open until 9pm. On Sunday opening hours are typically noon–5pm or 6pm. Many smaller, independently owned shops and Downtown businesses are closed on Sunday.

Sales Taxes

All purchases, except unprepared food and clothing less than $175 per item, are subject to 5 per cent state sales tax. Clothing over $175 is taxed on the excess amount. Accessories (including shoes and bags) are subject to the tax.

Boston's shopping comes in very manageable chunks. While the obvious places to head for Red Sox souvenirs and the like are beside Fenway Park and the tourist Mecca of Faneuil Hall-Quincy Market, those in search of less ubiquitous Boston products will not come away empty-handed by exploring other areas of the city.

BACK BAY

The widest and best range of shops are around Back Bay. Newbury Street offers the most pleasant retail experience and is renowned for its boutiques, art galleries, and quirky stores, particularly at the Massachusetts Avenue end. Luxury designer fashions, unique homewares, and the latest independent music are stocked at the ultra-chic Louis Boston (corner of Newbury and Berkeley streets). Down the street, Riccardi (no. 116) also caters to the hip crowd, with fashions fresh off the Milan runway. Root around The Closet (between Dartmouth and Exeter) for bargains on pre-loved high-end garments. John Fluevog (no. 302) carries trendy shoes to satisfy even the fussiest Imelda Marcos, while Johnny Cupcakes (no. 279) is the place for kooky cool T-shirts.

THE MALLS

On the corner of Boylston and Berkeley streets you will find Shreve, Crump & Low, Boston's answer to Tiffany's. Further along Boylston, the foot of the Prudential Tower is surrounded by the Prudential Center shopping mall (www.prudentialcenter.com; *see p.60*). This is connected via an enclosed footbridge to another mall, ritzy Copley Place (www.shopcopleyplace.com), where you will find Barneys, selling up-and-coming designers, and the fancy department store Neiman Marcus. Apart from all the expected chain stores, the Artful Hand Gallery has a superb selection of handmade artisan goods, great for unique souvenirs.

THE SOUTH END

One shopping area often overlooked by visitors is the South End. It is dotted with interesting independent shops and is a haven for art-lovers and epicureans. The epicenter of Boston's commercial contemporary art scene is Harrison Avenue *(see p.71)*. Here, Bernard Toale Gallery (at no. 450) has long been known for representing Boston's emerging talent. Next door, Bobbie

From Boston carries an impressive collection of vintage garments; it is rumored that designers from Ralph Lauren shop here for inspiration.

For modern design housewares, stop at Lekker on the corner of Washington and Waltham streets. The tempting aroma of scented candles wafts out of quirky Aunt Sadie's General Store at 18 Union Park Street. Around the block on Shawmut Avenue, Michele Mercaldo (no. 280) offers one-of-a-kind fine jewelry. Drop by Boston's best deli, South End Formaggio (no. 268), for free wine- and cheese-tasting.

BEACON HILL

This neighborhood is known for tradition and history, so it is no surprise that over 40 antiques shops have congregated here on Charles Street. Judith Dowling Asian Art at no. 133 specializes in Japanese decorative arts and functional objects; Eugene Galleries at no. 76 offers fine prints, etchings, and old maps, while at no. 38 E.R. Butler & Co. carries distinctive hardware and tableware inspired by historical designs.

HARVARD SQUARE

Over in Cambridge, despite many chain stores moving in, Harvard Square still maintains an academic atmosphere, with J. August and the Harvard Coop overflowing with Harvard insignia on everything. If the Coop does not stock the book you are after, chances are you will find it at one of the many other bookstores in the area, including Harvard Bookstore (1256 Massachusetts Avenue), specializing in used and remainders; Grolier (6 Plympton Street), offering America's largest poetry selection; Schoenhof's Foreign Books (76A Mount Auburn Street); and the children's bookstore Curious George Goes to Wordsworth (1 John F. Kennedy Street). Browsing the Museum of Useful Things on the corner of John F. Kennedy and Brattle streets is sure to turn up that useful something you never knew you needed.

DOWNTOWN AND WATERFRONT

While the Downtown location of Filene's Basement is temporarily closed *(see margin, right)*, Downtown Crossing's shopping is pretty much limited to Macy's and a few specialty stores. London Harness (60 Franklin Street) carries an impressive selection of luggage, and Bromfield Camera (10 Bromfield Street) has been serving photographers for almost 50 years.

Unsurprisingly, tourists love Faneuil Hall-Quincy Market *(see pp. 30 and 72)*, with over 100 local and national name stores gathered here. Check out Boston Pewter Company in the basement of Faneuil Hall, or the Bostonian Society Museum Shop in Quincy Market.

On the Waterfront shopping is limited, but this is changing as the area becomes more developed. For art books, objets d'art, and contemporary jewelry try the ICA *(see p. 75)*. The Achilles Project (283 Summer Street) offers limited-edition handcrafted garments.

Above from far left: Faneuil Hall Marketplace; kitted out in Red Sox gear; designer fashions on Newbury Street; Harvard is the place for books.

Filene's Redevelopment
There are plenty of stores along Downtown Crossing – the pedestrian precinct at the intersection of Washington, Summer, and Winter streets – but the temporary closure in September 2007 of the bargain-hunters' paradise Filene's Basement has put a dent in the area's bustle. Filene's site is being redeveloped in a $625 million project to include a 38-story tower, housing condominiums, a hotel, offices, and shops. It is slated to reopen in 2009, with promises that the bargain basement will still be there.

SPORTS AND ENTERTAINMENT

Baseball is king in Boston, with a city-wide devotion to the Red Sox, even though other sports teams are national champs too. The youthful student population also makes this a great place to party, with a diverse range of musical and theatrical offerings every night of the week.

Basketball Champs
For all the hoopla over the Red Sox, it is the Celtics who are the most successful team in any major sport in the country. Beginning in 1959, they won an unprecedented eight National Basketball Association (NBA) championships on the trot, and to date have 17 NBA wins to their credit.

Listings
Pick up a free copy of either *The Phoenix* (www.bostonphoenix.com) or *Weekly Dig* (www.weeklydig.com) to see who and what is playing around town, as well as for the low-down on the hottest clubs.

Right: Red Sox programs outside Fenway Park.

BASEBALL

Sports run in Boston's blood, and there is no more essential an element in that fluid than the Red Sox (www.redsox.com). In 2004 the city's Major League Baseball team finally broke the losing 'curse' in the World Series championships that had haunted them for 86 years – ever since the legendary slugger Babe Ruth was sold to eternal rivals, the New York Yankees. To prove their new-found form, the Red Sox snatched another World Series victory in 2007, much to the delight of Bostonians, who turned out en masse to welcome their heroes home in a tickertape parade.

OTHER SPORTS

The Red Sox can now stand proudly shoulder to shoulder with the city's American football team, the New England Patriots (www.patriots.com). Three-time winners of the Super Bowl, the Patriots came close to winning a fourth time in 2008. Their home ground is the Gillette Stadium at Foxborough, 32 miles (51.5km) south of Boston, and the season runs from late August to late December.

From October to mid-April at the T.D. Banknorth Garden Stadium (on Causeway Street above North Station), you can catch the games of the city's ice hockey team, the Bruins (www.bostonbruins.com), or the basketball team, the Celtics (www.nba.com/celtics).

CLASSICAL MUSIC, OPERA, AND BALLET

Offering everything from garage-band rock to orchestral works, Boston is one of the US's most musically diverse cities. For classical music, check out the concert schedule of the beautiful Symphony Hall (301 Massachusetts Avenue; tel: 617-266-1200; www.bso.

org), which hosts the world-class Boston Symphony Orchestra, founded in 1881, from November to May; the orchestra can also be heard occasionally playing outdoors at the Hatch Shell in the Esplanade *(see p.49)*, where you may also catch the Symphony's spin-off Boston Pops Orchestra (www.bostonpops.org).

Another excellent venue is Jordan Hall at the New England Conservatory of Music (30 Gainsborough Street; tel: 617-585-1260; www.newenglandcon servatory.edu), which stages many free concerts alongside ones by established ensembles, such as the Boston Philharmonic (www.bostonphil.org).

Opera, not Boston's strong point, is covered by the Boston Lyric Opera (www.blo.org) and the Boston Opera (www.operaboston.org). However, the Boston Ballet (bostonballet.org) is considered one of the top dance companies in the US.

ROCK AND POP

The stars of rock and pop regularly turn up at the city's biggest venues, such as the outdoor Bank of America Pavilion (May–Sept only) out on South Boston Waterfront, and T.D. Banknorth Garden (www.tdbank northgarden.com), or medium-sized spaces such as the shabby-chic Orpheum Theater (1 Hamilton Place; tel: 617-679-0810). However, with all those students around, there is an enormous range of small live music venues and a thriving indie rock scene of bands and singers to fill them.

Check out places such as T.T. the Bear's Place and Paradise Rock Club *(see pp.120–3 for nightlife listings, including pubs, live venues, and clubs).*

THEATER SCENE

Boston has a small but lively theater scene, with the city's grandest theaters, such as the Wang and the Shubert, often used for try-outs of Broadway-bound productions. The city's equivalent of *The Mousetrap* is the comic whodunnit *Shear Madness*, staged since 1980 at the Charles Playhouse (74 Warrenton Street; www.blueman.com), where you can also catch the long-running Blue Man Group.

The most reliable places for interesting productions are The American Repertory Theatre (Loeb Drama Center, 64 Brattle Street; www.amrep. org) over in Harvard, the Huntington (www.huntingtontheatre.org), and the South End's Boston Center for the Arts (www.bcaonline.org), which has four stages *(see also p.71).*

Above from far left: outdoor jazz session; theatrical performance at the Boston Center for the Arts; Boston Dragon Boat Festival on Charles River.

Half-price Tickets The Bostix booths beside Faneuil Hall (Tue–Sat 10am–6pm, Sun 11am–4pm) and on the corner of Copley Square (same hours; www.arts boston.org) sell half-price tickets for many events (cash only) on performance day.

The Boston Marathon

Since 1897, Patriot's Day – the third Monday in April – has seen city traffic come to a standstill for the running of the Boston Marathon (www.bostonmarathon.com), making this the world's oldest annually contested long-distance running race. That first 26-mile (42km) race began with just 15 participants, but today the marathon regularly has over 30,000 runners, including Olympic champions. The toughest section is the aptly named Heartbreak Hill, which rises up 80ft (24.3m) in the city's Newton Hills area. A half-marathon held in early October attracts around 5,000 runners.

HISTORY: KEY DATES

Settled by Native Americans for thousands of years before John Cabot claimed Massachusetts for King Henry VII of England in 1497, the Boston area is famous for its key role in American Independence.

PRE-REVOLUTIONARY BOSTON

Below: stained-glass window in the State House commemorating 1775; statue of Washington, the first president, in the Public Garden *(see p.55)*; detail from the Robert Gould Shaw Memorial, honoring the first regiment of freed blacks in the Civil War *(see p.50)*.

1625	William Blackstone, Boston's first colonist, settles on the Common.
1630	Puritan English settlers led by John Winthrop form Massachusetts Bay Company colony at Charlestown.
1635	Boston Latin School, the first public school in the nation, is founded.
1636	Harvard College is founded.
1684	Massachusetts Bay Company is made into a royal colony with a governor appointed by the king.
1692	The Salem Witch Trials begin.
1761	Boston lawyer James Otis declares: 'Taxation without representation is tyranny.'
1764	The Sugar Act and the Stamp Act arouse anti-royalist sentiments.

THE BATTLE FOR INDEPENDENCE

1770	Boston Massacre.
1773	Boston Tea Party.
1775	Paul Revere's ride and battles of Lexington and Concord spark the American Revolution. Battle of Bunker Hill and burning of Charlestown. George Washington assumes command of Continental Army at Cambridge.
1776	British troops withdraw from Massachusetts. Declaration of Independence is announced from State House.
1789	US Constitution is framed; John Hancock is declared first governor of state of Massachusetts.
1795	Paul Revere and Samuel Adams lay the cornerstone for the new State House designed by Charles Bulfinch on Beacon Hill.

19TH CENTURY

1812	War of 1812 against the British paralyzes the city's commerce.
1821	English High School, the first high school in the US, is opened.
1822	Boston is finally incorporated as a city.

1841	First Irish immigrants arrive.
1852	Charles McKim's Boston Public Library opens.
1857	Filling of Back Bay begins.
1861	Massachusetts Institute of Technology (MIT) granted charter.
1861–5	American Civil War.
1872	Great Fire of Boston.
1876	Salem resident Alexander Graham Bell patents the telephone.
1879	Mary Baker Eddy founds the Christian Science Church.
1881	Boston Symphony Orchestra is founded. Frederick Law Olmsted, landscape architect, begins work on Emerald Necklace park system.
1897	First Boston Marathon. America's first subway opens at Park Street.

Above from far left: detail from Paul Revere's engraving showing British troops opening fire in King Street in 1770; townsmen dressed as Indians dumping tea during the Boston Tea Party, 1773.

20TH CENTURY

1903	Boston is the site of first World Series – Red Sox win. First international wireless message transmitted by Guglielmo Marconi from Wellfleet on Cape Cod.
1910	A dam is built to form the Charles River Basin.
1915	Boston's first skyscraper is built.
1919	Strike of 1,300 Boston police. Breaking it brings to national prominence Massachusetts Governor Calvin Coolidge.
1946	John Fitzgerald Kennedy is elected Congressman for Charlestown and Cambridge.
1957	Boston Redevelopment Authority is launched by Mayor John Hynes.
1968	Completion of new City Hall.
1980s	The 'Massachusetts Miracle' high-tech revolution results in an economic boom.
1990	Thieves remove $200 million in paintings from Isabella Stewart Gardner Museum in the largest art heist in history.
1991	Start of the 'Big Dig' civic reconstruction.
1993	TV sitcom *Cheers*, set in a fictional Boston bar, ends after 275 episodes.
1996	The Harbor Islands are designated a national park area.

21ST CENTURY

2004	Red Sox break 87-year losing streak by winning World Series. The US's first legally recognized same-sex wedding takes place in Cambridge. Harvard students set up social networking site Facebook.
2006	Deval Patrick is elected Massachusetts governor, only the second black governor in the US.
2008	Boston Celtics win the NBA championships for the 17th time.

WALKS AND TOURS

BOSTON COMMON AND DOWNTOWN

Covering the first half of the historic Freedom Trail, this route runs from Boston Common, the city's geographical and social crossroads, through Downtown, to the oldest continuously run restaurant in the US.

Visitor Information
Boston's main Visitor Information Center (tel: 617-536-4100; www.bostonusa.com; daily 8.30am–5pm) is located on the northeastern edge of Boston Common, just south of the Park Street subway station (corner of Park and Tremont streets). You can pick up free maps and book tours here. It also serves as the beginning of the Freedom Trail *(see p.25).*

DISTANCE 1½ miles (2.5km)
TIME A half day
START Boylston T Station
END Haymarket T Station
POINTS TO NOTE

Downtown is busy with office workers Monday to Friday, particularly around lunchtime, so a good time to do this walk is early morning after rush hour or at the weekend. On Friday and Saturday there is also a lively fresh-produce market at Haymarket. If you do the walk in the afternoon, you could finish with dinner in Chinatown and a show in the Theater District.

Starting at Boston Common, one of the oldest sections of the city, and ending at the cobblestone streets of Blackstone Block, this walk will take you deep into Boston's history. During its 360-plus years the Common has been a popular spot for sermons, promenades, and, in the years before the Revolution, political protest. Stroll through it today and you will see everyone from Chinese women practicing t'ai chi in the shade of ancient elm trees to rappers and breakdancers showing off their skills, and office workers from Downtown's modern skyscrapers grabbing some fresh air while enjoying their lunch.

Chinatown and Theater District

Close to the walk's start, immediately east of Bolyston Street, are Boston's Chinatown and Theater District, areas you will likely want to return to for dining and evening entertainment. At the intersection of Surface Road and Beach Street (Chinatown's main drag) is an ornate *paifang*, a traditional-style Chinese gateway flanked by a pair of stone foo lions. The area around it has recently been landscaped into an attractive garden with bamboo and water features – a result of Downtown beautification after the Big Dig *(see p.13)*. Chinatown might not be large, but it is packed with lively Asian restaurants and exotic stores. It is great fun to visit, and can easily be combined with a night out at one of the theaters on Stuart or Tremont streets, such as the Wang and Shubert, where for decades Broadway-bound productions have had their trial runs.

Below: for dim sum head to Chinatown.

The Freedom Trail

Most of this route follows a section of the 2½-mile (4km) Freedom Trail. This runs through the heart of Boston past 16 significant sites that are among the city's oldest landmarks and featured in the decisive break that New England's settlers made from the British in 1776. Established in 1958 to preserve these key monuments and sites, the Trail is marked by a red-brick or painted line on the pavement. It is relatively easy to follow, but if you would prefer to have a guided tour, **The Freedom Trail Foundation** (tel: 617-357-8300; www.thefreedomtrail.org) offers daily tours from the Visitor Information Center on Boston Common (see margin, left).

BOSTON COMMON

This walk starts at the southeast corner of **Boston Common**, at the junction of Boylston and Tremont streets. The Common, established in 1634, is the oldest public park in the US and a storybook of Boston history. Originally used as a 'Comon Field' (sic) on which sheep and cattle grazed (they did so up until 1830), the pentagonal space, covering about 50 acres (20ha), was also used as a mustering ground for militias and a venue for public hangings. Among those who met a cruel end dangling from the Great Elm, which stood on the Common until 1876, were Mary Dyer, the heroic Quaker who insisted on the right to worship freely. A statue in her memory stands outside the State House on the corner of Beacon and Bowdon streets (see margin, p.51).

Central Burying Ground

Immediately to the left as you face the Common from the corner of Boylston Street is the **Central Burying Ground** ❶ (daily dawn–dusk). During the American Revolution the Common was transformed into a British military center. As many as 2,000 Redcoats were quartered here during Boston's occupation, and several dozen British

Above from far left: shady spot on Boston Common; Freedom Trail pavement sign; tour guide in period costume; Cutler Majestic Theatre in the Theater District.

soldiers killed at the Battle of Bunker Hill were interred in the cemetery. It is the city's fourth-oldest cemetery, but few of note are buried here. One exception is Gilbert Stuart (1755–1828) who painted the classic portrait of George Washington *(see p.65).*

Soldiers and Sailors Monument

The western part of the Common is devoted to athletic endeavor, with a well-patronized baseball field and tennis courts. Head north from the burying ground, watching out for scampering grey squirrels, past the pretty Parkman Bandstand, to admire the 70ft (21m) **Soldiers and Sailors Monument ❷**, located atop Telegraph Hill. It is dedicated to the Union forces killed in the Civil War.

Frog Pond

Close by is **Frog Pond ❸**, used as a children's wading pool in summer and an ice rink in winter. In colonial times sheep and cows slaked their thirst at this watering hole. Later, Bostonians fished in it for minnows in the summer and ice-skated on it in the winter, and here they celebrated the first arrival of piped-in municipal water from a suburban reservoir in 1848. Sadly, lined with concrete today, the pond is no longer a home for minnows nor frogs.

PARK STREET

Exit the Common at its northeast corner on Park Street. If you fancy some lunch at this point, you can backtrack a little from here southeast down Tremont Street and left into Temple Place to find **Ivy**, see ⑪①.

Just north of Park Street T Station, on the corner of Park and Tremont streets, stands **Park Street Church ❹** (tel: 617-523-3383; www.parkstreet. org; mid-June–Aug Tue–Sat 9.30am–3.30pm; free), with its majestic 217ft (66m) steeple (adapted from a Christopher Wren design). William Lloyd Garrison delivered his first anti-slavery speech here in 1829.

OLD GRANARY BURYING GROUND

Next to the church, on Tremont Street, pay your respects at the grave of Paul Revere, Samuel Adams, John Hancock, and other key revolutionary figures in the illustrious **Old Granary Burying Ground ❺** (9am–5pm, winter until 3pm), dating from 1660. The graveyard is named after the granary that was

---

Taking a Trolley

Several sightseeing 'trolleys' (in fact, conventional wheeled vehicles with trolley-like bodywork) run at roughly 15-minute intervals on routes around Boston's main sights. It is a great way to get to know the city, especially if time is limited. You can hop off wherever you like, explore on foot, and then board a later trolley – just make sure the trolley company matches your ticket. Operators include Old Town Trolley Tours (tel: 617-269-7010; www.trolleytours.com/Boston), City View Trolley Tours (tel: 617-363-7899; www.city viewtrolleys.com), and Brush Hill Tours (tel: 617-720-6342; www.brushhilltours.com).

demolished to make way for the Park Street Church. Opposite is **KO Prime**, see ⑪②.

OMNI PARKER HOUSE HOTEL

Continue to the corner of School and Tremont, past the fancy Venetian facade of the Tremont Temple Baptist Church (once a famous Boston theater), where stands the **Omni Parker House Hotel ❻**, the oldest continuously operating hotel in the US. The present building is not the original, but much of the lobby's ornately carved wooden decoration is. Pop inside to see where Charles Dickens conducted literary seminars, the Vietnamese leader Ho Chi Minh waited on tables, and Malcolm X toiled in the kitchen. The hotel lays claim to inventing a couple of Boston's culinary favourites – Boston cream pie and the Parker Roll, a soft bread roll.

KING'S CHAPEL AND BURYING GROUND

On the corner of School and Tremont streets is **King's Chapel ❼** (tel: 617-523-1749; www.kings-chapel.org; July–Aug daily 10am–4pm, other months Sat 10am–4pm, Sun 1.30–4pm; services Wed 12.15pm and Sun 11am). The present granite structure dates from 1754, but the chapel had its origins in the 1680s, when Britain's King James II made a colossal political blunder by sending to Boston a clergyman whose job was to install in the town the very thing the Puritans had hated and fled: a branch of the Church of England.

Next to the Chapel, on Tremont Street, is Boston's first cemetery, **King's Chapel Burying Ground** (daily 9am–5pm, winter until 3pm), in use from 1630 to 1796, thus predating the Anglican edifice whose name it later assumed. The Bay Colony's first

Above from far left: Parkman Bandstand; Omni Parker House Hotel; King's Chapel and Burying Ground.

The Historic T
Opened in 1897, 'Park Street Under' was the first subway station in the US. The subway now falls under the auspices of the Massachusetts Bay Transport Authority (MBTA; see pp.104–6). Most Bostonians simply call it 'The T,' after the system's logo: a T in a circle.

Below left: Park Street Church.

Food and Drink

① IVY
49 Temple Place; tel: 617-451-1416; www.ivyrestaurantgroup.com; Mon–Thur 11am–3pm, Mon–Wed 5–11pm, Thur 5pm–midnight, Fri 11am–midnight, Sat 4pm–midnight, Sun 4–11pm; $$
Stylish modern restaurant and bar serving simple lunches and small plates for dinner that are designed to share. Buzzes after work hours when young professionals stop in for a drink.

② KO PRIME
Nine Zero Hotel, 90 Tremont Street; tel: 617-772-0202; www.koprimeboston.com; Mon–Fri 6.30–10.30am, 11.30am–2pm, 5.30–10pm, Sat 8am–2pm, 5.30–10pm, Sun 8am–2pm, 5.30–9.30pm; $$$
Chef Ken Oringer's stylish steakhouse, decorated with cow hide, emphasizes farm-fresh produce, including grass-fed Kobe and Wagyu beef, and seafood. The wine list is extensive.

Ticket Saving
If you plan to enter
the Old South
Meeting House, the
Old State House, and
Paul Revere House
(see p.33), then it is
worth buying a
combined discount
ticket for $11. The
ticket is sold at each
of the places and can
be used any time.

Below: Old South
Meeting House.

governor, John Winthrop, was buried
here in 1649.

The monument at the corner of the
burying ground honors a French naval
adjutant, the Chevalier de Saint-
Sauveur, killed by a Boston mob in
September 1778 during an altercation
over bread. The French, who had come
to help the colonials, were baking
bread using their own stores of wheat;
Bostonians, who were enduring a
severe shortage of flour, were incensed
when told that they could not buy the
French Navy's bread. The Chevalier's
funeral service is said to have been the
first Catholic Mass in Boston.

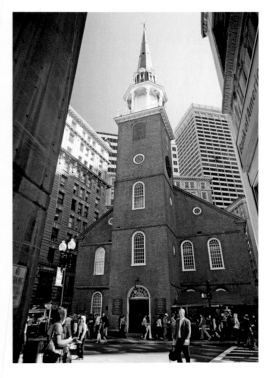

OLD CITY HALL

Further down School Street is **Old
City Hall ❽** (tel: 617-523-8678;
www.oldcityhall.com), built in 1865 in
the French Second Empire style.
When the city government decamped
from here in 1969 for the new City
Hall *(see p.30)*, this handsome edifice
was preserved as a mixed-use complex
of offices and a restaurant: the current
tenant is the pricey chain Ruth's Chris
Steak House (tel: 617-742-8401).

In the forecourt are bronze statues
of Benjamin Franklin and Josiah
Quincy, in his time a senator, Boston
mayor, and president of Harvard. Pop
into the hall's vestibule to read about
the building's history and that of the
Boston Latin School, the nation's first
school, which once stood close to this
spot – hence the name School Street.
Look down the sidewalk outside and
you will see a pretty hopscotch mosaic
celebrating the school.

OLD CORNER BOOKSTORE

Continue to the intersection of School
and Washington streets, where you
will find the **Old Corner Bookstore
❾**, dating from 1712, and currently a
jeweler's. Over the years the building
has served as an apothecary, a dry-
goods store, and private residence,
although it is fondly remembered in its
1828 incarnation as the home of the
eminent Ticknor and Fields publishing firm and a bookstore. In the
Golden Age of American literature the
store was a popular meeting place for

Whittier, Emerson, Stowe, Alcott, and other distinguished writers.

In the small square opposite stands the **Irish Famine Memorial**, which honors the 37,000 Irish who emigrated to America in the mid-19th century in the wake of Ireland's potato famine.

OLD SOUTH MEETING HOUSE

Immediately to the right on Washington Street is the **Old South Meeting House** ⑩ (tel: 617-482-6439; www.oldsouthmeetinghouse. org; daily Apr–Oct 9.30am–5pm, Nov–Mar 10am–4pm; charge), built in 1727 and styled after the graceful London chapels of Sir Christopher Wren. The church was the scene of the events that preceded the infamous Boston Tea Party of 1773 and the baptism on a chilly January 6, 1706, of Benjamin Franklin, born around the corner on Milk Street, where you will find the **Milk Street Café**, see ⑪③, a good-value choice for lunch.

OLD STATE HOUSE

From the Old South Meeting House, continue north along Washington Street toward the junction with State Street. Immediately to the right, overshadowed by modern skyscrapers, is the **Old State House** ⑪ (tel: 617-720-3290; www.bostonhistory.org; daily 9am–5pm, June–late Aug until 6pm; charge), Boston's oldest public building, built in 1713 as the seat of the colonial government, and now a small museum. In 1787 John Hancock was inaugurated here as the first governor of the state under its new Constitution. You can recognize the building by those symbols of British imperial power, the lion and unicorn, the originals of which were thrown into the street when the Declaration of Independence was read from the balcony on July 18, 1776. On display inside are items relating to Boston's role in the Revolutionary War and other parts of the city's history.

NATIONAL PARK SERVICE VISITOR CENTER

Opposite the Old State House is the **National Park Service Visitor Center** (15 State Street; tel: 617-242-5642; www.nps.gov/bost; daily 9am–5pm), a valuable source of information and literature from which Rangers lead free daily walking tours along part of the Freedom Trail; see the website for details. For a healthy lunch or snack, try nearby **Sebastians**, see ⑪④ *(see p.31)*, at 1 Devonshire Place.

Above from far left: guide in colonial dress; clock atop the Old State House; Irish Famine Memorial.

Boston Tea Party
It was on December 16, 1773, at the Old South Meeting House, that more than 5,000 Bostonians met to decide what to do with three tea-laden ships in the harbor. Disguised as Mohawk Indians, a gang of colonists, enraged at the British tax placed on tea and other imports, ran down Milk Street to Griffins Wharf. The crowd followed, and, with cries of 'Boston harbor a teapot tonight!', 340 crates of tea were dumped overboard.

Food and Drink 🍴
③ MILK STREET CAFÉ
50 Milk Street; tel: 617-542-3663; http://milkstreetcafe.com; Mon–Fri 7am–3pm; $
Reasonable prices for generous portions is the deal at this kosher cafeteria, with dairy and fish, no meats. Made-from-scratch dishes, such as roasted salmon salad and vegetable lasagne, and nutritious homemade soups.

Below: period outfit in the Old State House.

Above from left:
stark Boston City
Hall; seafood
institution on Union
Street; New England
Holocaust Memorial.

BOSTON MASSACRE

Continuing along the Freedom Trail
from the Old State House, it is easy
to miss the circle of cobblestones on
a tiny traffic island at the junction of
State and Congress streets. This marks
the spot of the **Boston Massacre** ⑫
where, on March 5, 1770, a handful
of British soldiers fired into a jeering
crowd that was pelting them with
snowballs; five men were killed,
including former slave Crispus
Attucks, who is buried in the Old
Granary Burying Ground *(see p.26)*.

FANEUIL HALL

Head north on Congress Street and
turn right to reach **Faneuil Hall** ⑬

Below: Faneuil Hall.

(tel: 617-242-5642; www.faneuilhall.
com; daily 9.30am–4.30pm; free). A
statue of Samuel Adams, one of the
Founding Fathers of the United
States, stands in front of the former
public hall, which was named after
benefactor Peter Faneuil. Designated
by patriot orator James Otis as the
'Cradle of Liberty,' it was here that
the Sons of Liberty called many meetings of complaint about British
taxation without representation.

On the building's lower floors are
many touristy shops, more of which
you will find in the adjacent Quincy
Market complex: browse them now or
during walk 10 *(see p.72)*.

BOSTON CITY HALL

On the western side of Congress
Street, climb the concrete steps
leading up to **Boston City Hall** ⑭.
Prior to the construction in 1969 of
this charmless inverted ziggurat, the
area was known as Scollay Square, a
slightly disreputable entertainment
area. In the 1960s the Boston Redevelopment Authority decided to
raze Scollay Square and the nearby
tenements of the West End. The area
was renamed Government Center, its
focus the vast, empty, and depressing
City Hall Plaza.

NEW ENGLAND
HOLOCAUST MEMORIAL

Also far from uplifting, but beautiful
in a melancholy way, are the six tall,
slender glass-and-steel towers of the

New England Holocaust Memorial in Carmen Park, a strip of greenery opposite the City Hall between Union and Congress streets. Forming a mute tribute to the those murdered by the Nazis in World War II, each glass column, wreathed in steam symbolizing the gas chambers, represents a different concentration camp and is inscribed with numbers – 6 million in total.

At the Faneuil Hall end of the park are two bronze statues of James Curley, the Irish politician who dominated Boston politics from 1920 to 1950, even managing to be re-elected while in jail.

BLACKSTONE BLOCK

In stark contrast to the concrete wastelands of Government Center are the charming brick buildings and cobbled lanes, dating back to the 17th century, of **Blackstone Block ⓯**, named after Boston's first colonist, William Blackstone (who settled in the Boston Common area in 1625). The block is bounded by Union, Hanover, Blackstone, and North streets. At 41 Union Street is the historic **Union Oyster House**, see ⓘⓢ.

A few yards down Marshall Street (just off Union Street), opposite the 18th-century Ebenezer Hancock House at no. 10, look down to see the **Boston Stone**, a stone ball and stone trough built into the wall of a gift shop. Shipped from England in 1700 to serve as a paint mill, the stones were later used as the point from

which all distances from Boston were measured. Their role as the hub of 'The Hub' was later taken over by the dome of the Massachusetts State House *(see p.51)*.

If it is Friday or Saturday, you might want to linger around here to enjoy the **fresh produce market** that wraps its way around North and Blackstone streets.

Otherwise, return to Congress Street, at the head of which is **Haymarket Station**, where you can finish this tour, or catch the T back to Boylston or Chinatown stations for dinner and a night at the theater *(see p.24)*. Alternatively, continue across the Rose Kennedy Greenway park into the North End for the second half of the Freedom Trail *(see p.32)*.

Food and Drink 🍴

④ SEBASTIANS
1 Devonshire Place, Congress Street; tel: 617-624-7979; www.sebastians.com/cafes; Mon–Fri 7am–4pm; $
Local café chain serving tasty made-to-order salads, sandwiches, and daily lunch specials. It is a popular lunch spot with health-conscious office workers.

⑤ UNION OYSTER HOUSE
41 Union Street; tel: 617-227-2750; www.unionoysterhouse.com; Sun–Thur 11am–9.30pm, Fri–Sat 11am–10pm; $$
A favorite haunt of President Kennedy, this touristy restaurant has a top-class raw bar, and serves both seafood and steaks in atmospheric rooms with creaky floors, low ceilings, and wooden booths.

Ye Olde House
Union Oyster House claims the title of Boston's oldest brick house. A rare example of Georgian architecture in the city, the restaurant dates from at least 1660, when it was owned by Boston's first town crier, William Courser. Mentioned in a city plan of 1708, the house was the office of the *Massachusetts Spy* newspaper from 1771 to 1775, while in 1796 the exiled Louis-Philippe, who later became king of France, taught French in the rooms above James Amblard's tailor shop.

THE NORTH END AND CHARLESTOWN

The second half of the Freedom Trail traverses the North End and Charlestown, two of Boston's oldest settled areas, packed with historical sites and great places to eat and drink. The North End, Boston's Little Italy, is an especially pleasant place to return to in the evening for a meal.

Above: snapshots of Boston's Little Italy.

DISTANCE 2½ miles (4.5km)
TIME A half day
START Haymarket T Station
END Community College T Station
POINTS TO NOTE

This walk follows on from the end of walk 1, and the two can be linked for a full day's itinerary. An alternative way to access or leave this walk is by hopping on the Inner Harbor Ferry, which connects Charlestown Navy Yard with Long Wharf beside the Aquarium *(see p.74)*. Ferries run daily, every 30 minutes on the quarter of the hour, between 6.30am and 8pm, and cost $1.70.

Much of the North End's charm as a neighborhood comes from its improvisational quality, with a hodgepodge of buildings – some quite attractive, others not, and many dating from the late 1800s, when they were used as tenement houses for European immigrants.

Hanover Street is the area's main thoroughfare, but around it spreads an archaic and confusing street plan. The North End is one of those places where it is easy to get lost, and probably best that you do. All kinds of unconventional spaces, not to mention many delicious delis, cafés, and restaurants can be discovered in the neighborhood's less traveled areas.

ROSE KENNEDY GREENWAY

Begin the walk at **Haymarket T Station**. Until only a few years ago the raised expanse of the Fitzgerald Expressway (also known as the Central Artery) cut the North End off from the rest of the city. Now that the Big Dig has buried the road underground *(see feature, p.13)*, the cleared land forms a ribbon of parks through the city, known collectively as the **Rose Kennedy Greenway**. Rose Fitzgerald Kennedy, mother of President John F. Kennedy, was born in the North End in 1890, and her funeral was conducted at St Stephen's Church *(see p.34)* on Hanover Street in 1995.

HANOVER STREET

Head southeast through the park until you reach Hanover Street. On either side, as the street cuts through the park, are railings inscribed with historical dates and quotations about the area from past residents.

Refreshment Options

As Hanover Street enters the North End it is almost wall-to-wall with cafés and restaurants. For an espresso to power your way stop at **Caffé Paradiso**, see ⑪①. A bit further along the street, **Caffé Vittoria**, see ⑪②, and **The Daily Catch**, see ⑪③, are also recommended.

PAUL REVERE HOUSE

Turn right on Richmond Street and then left to enter cobbled North Square, where at no. 19 is the **Paul Revere House ❶** (tel: 617-523-2338; www.paulreverehouse.org; daily mid-Apr–Oct 9.30am–5.15pm, Nov–mid-Apr 9.30am–4.15pm; charge). Built in

Above from far left: view of the North End from St Stephen's Church to the Old North Church; Paul Revere House; Italian fare abounds in the North End.

Food and Drink 🍴

① CAFFÉ PARADISO
255 Hanover Street; tel: 617-742-1768; www.caffeparadiso.com; daily 6.30am–2am; $$
A popular local hangout, this café's espresso, cannoli, panini, and calzoni are particularly delicious. The TV beams in soccer games from Italy via satellite.

② CAFFÉ VITTORIA
290–296 Hanover Street; tel: 617-227-7606; www.vittoriacaffe.com; daily 6am–midnight; $
A quintessential Italian café, with quirky decor that includes almost a museum's worth of antique espresso machines. All kinds of other beverages are also served, along with traditional sweets.

③ THE DAILY CATCH
323 Hanover Street; tel: 617-523-8567; www.dailycatch.com; Sun–Thur 11am–10pm, Fri–Sat 11am–11pm; $
A tiny hole-in-the-wall institution that specializes in Sicilian seafood. There is also another branch at Fan Pier, 2 Northern Avenue (tel: 617-772-4400; handy for walk 10 (see p.74).

1680, this two-story dwelling, with an overhanging second floor, is the oldest wooden house in downtown Boston. Revere, then a silversmith, took up residence in 1770, and the house is furnished today much as it was when it was home to him and the first Mrs Revere, who bore him eight children, and then, when she died, to the second Mrs Revere, who produced a similar brood. It is from here that Revere started his historic horse ride that warned, 'the British are coming!'

Pierce-Hichborn House

Next door is the restored **Pierce-Hichborn House** (open for guided tours only once or twice daily; call Paul Revere House for details), which belonged to Nathaniel Hichborn, Revere's cousin. The asymmetrical,

Right: St Stephen's Church steeple.

three-story brick building, built between 1711 and 1715 in the new English Renaissance style, was a radical departure from the Tudor-style wooden dwellings built in the previous century.

ST STEPHEN'S CHURCH

Exit North Square via Prince Street, following the red bricks of the Freedom Trail back to Hanover Street. Turn right and walk two blocks north to reach **St Stephen's Church ❷**, with its white steeple. Built in 1804 as a Congregationalist Meeting House, this dignified structure is the only one of five Boston churches designed by Charles Bulfinch *(see p.12)* that still stands. In 1813 it became a Unitarian church, and in 1862 it was acquired by the Roman Catholic archbishopric. Eight years later, when Hanover Street had to be widened to accommodate traffic, the church was moved back 12ft (3.7m) and raised 6ft (1.8m); then, in 1965, it was restored to its original level.

PAUL REVERE MALL

Directly opposite St Stephen's Church is the **Paul Revere Mall**, known locally as the Prado. Built in 1933, this spacious brick courtyard is one of the liveliest public spaces in the North End – a sort of Americanized piazza where kids run around, old folks play cards, and footsore tourists take a breather from the Freedom Trail. In addition to a traditional

Italian fountain, the Prado features a magnificent equestrian statue of Paul Revere, modeled in 1885 by Cyrus Dallin and cast in 1940. On the southern (left) wall, bronze panels recall the history of Boston and its people.

OLD NORTH CHURCH

At the far end of the Prado a small gate opens to the rear of Christ Church, more popularly known as **Old North Church** ❸ (tel: 617-523-6676; www.oldnorth.com; June–Oct daily 9am–6pm, Nov–May Mon–Sat 9am–5pm, Sun 9–9.45am, 10.45am–12.15pm; free). Before going into the church, take note on the left of the three-story (originally it was two) brick home of Ebenezer Clough, built in 1712. Next to it is a small garden planted as it would have been in the 18th century, while opposite is a poignant reminder of a more modern event: a Memorial Garden hung with military dog tags for those who have perished in recent wars in Afghanistan and Iraq.

Interior

Built in 1723, Old North is Boston's oldest church. Its interior, painted white since 1912, sports high pew boxes, designed to keep in the warmth of braziers filled with hot coal or bricks, which were placed on the floor on wintry days. The clock at the rear of the church and the four baroque Belgian cherubs that surround it date back to the opening of the church. So does the organ case, although the

actual instrument dates only from 1759. It is still played at the service every Sunday at 11am.

The bust of George Washington, in a niche to the left of the apse, was the first public memorial to the great man, and was said by General Lafayette in 1824 to be 'more like him than any other portrait.' Another historical artifact is the 'third' steeple lantern, lit by President Gerald Ford during the American bicentennial observance at the church in 1975. The church has 37 crypts, containing, it is claimed, 1,100 bodies.

Above from far left:
Old North Church inside and out.

North End History

On colonial maps the North End looks like an irregular thumb jutting into the Atlantic Ocean, with a canal, called the Mill Stream, cutting it off from the larger Shawmut Peninsula.

By the late colonial period the small cluster of wooden houses had become one of Boston's most fashionable quarters, with several fine brick homes and some of the richest families in town. Unfortunately, many of the prominent residents were Tories who, when the British evacuated in 1776, hightailed it to Canada and took their money with them. Rich Yankees pulled out too, preferring the more genteel atmosphere of Beacon Hill, then being developed. Artisans, sailors, and tradesmen filled the empty houses, and throughout the 19th century the North End was a working man's quarter dominated by the shipping industry.

The Irish poured into the neighborhood in the 1840s, and soon dominated the area politically. Eastern European Jews followed the Irish, and by 1890 had established a thriving residential and business district along Salem Street. The Italians – mostly from Sicily and the southern provinces of the mainland – were the last group to arrive in substantial numbers; by the 1920s they had established an overwhelming majority, and have dominated the neighborhood ever since.

COPP'S HILL BURYING GROUND

Exit from the church, and walk northwest up Hull Street for about 150yds/m to **Copp's Hill Burying Ground** ❹ (daily dawn–dusk), Boston's second-oldest cemetery (after King's Chapel; *see p.27*), where the gravestones, some ornately carved, poke out of the grass like misshapen teeth. Its name comes from that of William Copp, who farmed on the hill's southeast slope in the mid-17th century. In the colonial era, the base of the hill, known pejoratively as New Guinea (after the African country of Guinea), was occupied by the city's first black community, and about 1,000 black citizens are buried in the cemetery's northwest corner.

Notable Tombstones

In the graveyard's northeast corner a tall black monument commemorates Prince Hall, who helped found Boston's first school for black children, and who was also the founder, in 1784, of the African Grand Lodge of Massachusetts, the world's first black Masonic Lodge. Nearby is the tombstone of 'Capt. Daniel Malcolm, Mercht,' who is remembered for smuggling 60 casks of wine into port without paying the duty. He asked to be buried 'in a Stone Grave 10 feet deep,' secure from desecration. His body may have been safe, but his tombstone was not: on it are scars made by the Redcoats who singled it out for target practice.

Weekend Processions

If you are in Boston in summer, be sure to time your visit to the North End to catch one of the Italian community's local feasts, or *festas*, celebrated in honor of saints' days. They are held almost every weekend in July and August, with Sunday being by far the more exciting day, and usually involve street fairs, brass bands, singers, raffles, food stalls selling sausage and peppers and *zeppole* (fried dough), and processions in which saints' statues are carried, often festooned with contributions of paper money. In the Feast of the Madonna del Soccorso (Our Lady of Succor), celebrated in mid-August, the star of the show is the famous flying angel. Portrayed by a little girl on a pulley, she floats above North Street, her arms outstretched to the crowd, and is lowered to the statue and the procession below. The biggest celebrations are the Fisherman's Feast and St Anthony's Feast in late August.

Food and Drink 🍴

④ SORELLE BAKERY AND CAFÉ

100 City Square, Charlestown; tel: 617-242-2125; www.sorellecafe. com; Mon–Fri 7am–7pm, Sat 8am–7pm, Sun 8am–5pm; $
This new branch (the original is at 1 Monument Avenue) keeps longer hours and has trendier looks, but still serves incredible breads and pastries, plus fresh sandwiches and salads.

CHARLESTOWN

The Freedom Trail's red-brick route leads you along Hull Street to Commercial Street, where you turn left and then right to cross the Charles River on the **Charlestown Bridge ❺**.

Ahead lies the city's oldest settlement, established in 1628, two years ahead of Boston. In 1630 it was the seat of the British government, and on its Breed's Hill the bloody Battle of Bunker Hill was fought on June 17, 1775. The area's prosperity was later tied up with the Navy Yard founded in 1800. At times (usually wartimes), it was the busiest shipbuilding and repair yard in the US, but in 1974 demand slowed to the point where the facility was forced to close – a third of it was taken over by the National Park Service.

Crossing the bridge (don't look down if you suffer from vertigo – the water seems awfully close through the metal grill) provides an excellent view on the left of the **Charlestown Locks**, which control the water level between the river and the Inner Harbor, and, rising majestically in the background, the **Leonard P. Zakim Bunker Hill Bridge** (www.leonardpzakimbunkerhillbridge. org), one of the most striking contemporary structures in the city.

Paul Revere Park

Below the bridge on the Charlestown side of the river is pretty little **Paul Revere Park ❻**, part of the Harbor-Walk *(see feature, p.75)*. Take the steps down to the park and follow the walkway under the Charlestown Bridge and past the hotel on Tudor Wharf toward the Charlestown Navy Yard.

City Square

Before exploring the Charlestown Navy Yard, you could take a breather at **Sorelle Bakery and Café**, see ⑪④, facing onto **City Square**, to the northwest. In the square's center a small circle of greenery preserves the foundations of the Great House, dating from 1629 and believed to have been John Winthrop's home and the colony's brief seat of government. The house became the Three Cranes Tavern in 1635, and was destroyed during the Battle of Bunker Hill.

CHARLESTOWN NAVY YARD

Walk for 100yds/m or so along Constitution Road toward the entrance of **Charlestown Navy Yard ❼**, whose most famous resident is the USS *Constitution (see p.38)*. Just inside the entrance is the new **Visitor Center** (tel: 617-242-5601; www.nps.gov/bost; daily Sept–June 9am–5pm, July–Aug 9am–6pm), where you can find out about free tours of the ship and its neighbor, the restored naval destroyer USS *Cassin Young*, which served in the Pacific during World War II. Elsewhere in the National Park Service-administered area you can wander around the old buildings and dry docks used to mend ships. Escape the crowds at the little-visited **Massachusetts Korean War Veterans Memorial**, where you can listen to recordings of veterans remembering the conflict.

Above from far left:
Copp's Hill gravestones; clapboard houses in the Bunker Hill neighborhood.

Narrow House
Opposite the main entrance to Copp's Hill Burying Ground, take note of the gray-painted clapboard house at 44 Hull Street. At just 9½ft (3m) wide, this is Boston's narrowest home, allegedly built around 1800 by a spiteful man to block the light coming into the neighboring house.

USS Constitution

Boston-built and first sailed from here in 1797, the **USS Constitution** ❽ (www.ussconstitution.navy.mil; Apr–Oct Tue–Sun, Nov–Mar Thur–Sun 10am–3.30pm; tours on the half-hour) is the world's oldest warship still in commission. It keeps this status thanks to an annual July 4 'turnaround,' when tugs pull it out into the harbor.

On board, Navy enlistees in 1812 uniform conduct guided tours and answer questions. During the busy summer months lines to tour the USS *Constitution* can be long.

Opposite the ship is the **USS *Constitution* Museum** ❾ (tel: 617-426-1812; www.ussconstitutionmuseum.org; daily mid-Apr–mid-Oct 9am–6pm, mid-Oct–mid-Apr 10am–5pm; free, but donations welcome), which simulates the experience of life below decks. You can place your hands on a ship's wheel, climb into a hammock, or hoist the sail on a moving 'deck' while the sounds of shipboard life echo all around. Also on show in the museum is a walk-through model of a keel and ribbing, and a continuous audiovisual program that depicts a bloody sea battle of 1812.

BUNKER HILL MONUMENT AND MUSEUM

Exit the Navy Yard back onto Constitution Road and turn right to reach Chelsea Street. Duck through the nearby underpass beneath the Tobin Bridge, emerging on Lowney Way. Turn left and then immediately right onto Chestnut Street. Continue along Chestnut Street to the **Bunker Hill Monument** ❿ (daily 9am–4.30pm; free), a 220ft (67m) high granite obelisk crowning Breed's Hill. The battle was fought just north of the monument.

Climb the 294 stairs to the top for rewarding views of the city. The bronze statue on a pedestal in front of the monument is Colonel William Prescott, the patriot who uttered the immortal line, 'Don't fire until you see the whites of their eyes!' as an instruction to the troops before the battle.

On the corner of Monument Square and Monument Avenue is the

Old Ironsides

During its active service between 1797 and 1855 the USS *Constitution* was a victor in 42 battles. According to legend, it was during an engagement with the British warship *Guerrière* in 1812 that the *Constitution* earned the sobriquet 'Old Ironsides'; on seeing the enemy's cannonballs apparently bouncing off the boat's side, a sailor exclaimed: 'Her sides are made of iron!' The real reason behind the nickname is more mundane: the *Constitution* was constructed of live oak, which is said to be five times more durable than white oak.

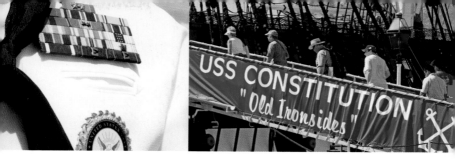

small **Battle of Bunker Hill Museum** (tel: 617-242-5641; www.nps.gov/bost; daily 9am–5pm; free), where, on the second floor, hangs an excellent reproduction of the *Bunker Hill Cyclorama*, a circular painting that places the viewer at the heart of the battle's action. The original was shown in 1888 at the now demolished Castle Square Theater at 421 Tremont Street in the South End.

WINTHROP SQUARE

From the southeast corner of Monument Square head downhill along Winthrop Street, which leads into picturesque **Winthrop Square ⑪**. For a century this was a training field where Charlestown boys learned the art of war. At the northwest corner is a gate flanked by bronze tablets commemorating those killed on June 17, 1775.

Refreshment Options
Return to Winthrop Street and keep going downhill, past the fire station and across Warren Street until you reach the junction with Main Street. Turn right here to find the gourmet pizzeria **Figs**, see ⑪⑤, or a couple of blocks further on the corner of Pleasant Street, the historic **Warren Tavern**, see ⑪⑥, dating from 1780. Both Paul Revere and George Washington once stayed here.

SAVINGS BANK BUILDING

A few yards north, where Main Street meets Austin Street, stands the handsome Victorian Gothic-style **Savings**

Bank Building ⑫ at 1 Thompson Square, built in 1876. The interior has been sensitively adapted into offices, a florist, barber, and café, with the bank's enormous vaults still left in tact.

From here a short walk west along Austin Street and across busy Rutherford Avenue will bring you to **Community College Station**, behind Bunker Hill Community College, the end of this route.

Alternatively, amble back through Charlestown, admiring its many old homes, toward the Navy Yard to pick up the Inner Harbor Ferry to Long Wharf *(see box, p.32)*.

(see box, p.32)

Food and Drink 🍴

⑤ FIGS
67 Main Street; tel: 617-242-2229; Mon–Thur 5.30–10pm, Fri 5.30–10.30pm, Sat 5–10.30pm, Sun 4.30–9pm; $$
Celebrity chef Todd English's gourmet pizzeria serves the excellent thin-crust pizza grilled in wood-fired ovens and topped with a variety of epicurean toppings. The fig and prosciutto special is a perennial favorite. There's a second location at 24 Charles Street, Beacon Hill, tel: 617-742-3447, good for walk 5 *(see p.50)*.

⑥ WARREN TAVERN
2 Pleasant Street; tel: 617-241-8142; www.warrentavern.com; Mon–Fri 11.30am–1am, Sat–Sun 10.30am–1am; $
Named after revolutionary hero General Warren, this historic pub has low ceilings and beams, making it a convivial spot for lunch. Burgers and chunky sandwiches are the specialty. Live music some evenings.

Above from far left: Bunker Hill Monument; naval uniform; all aboard the USS *Constitution*.

Below: historic watering hole.

HARVARD

World-famous Harvard University is actually in the separate city of Cambridge, which lies on the north bank of the Charles River. This walking tour takes you around the university's hallowed halls, into some of its excellent museums, and back across the river for fantastic views.

DISTANCE 4 miles (6.5km)
TIME A full day including museum visits
START/END Harvard Square T Station
POINTS TO NOTE
It is difficult to do full justice to all of Harvard's museums in one day. Decide whether you would prefer a brief once-over of everything, or a concentrated session at, say, the natural history museums. Note that the Fogg Art and Busch-Reisinger Museums are closed until 2013 while a new building is being constructed (see margin, p.43).

Below: 'The Statue of the Three Lies'; Harvard flag; rhino outside Harvard's Biological Laboratories.

HARVARD YARD

Emerging from **Harvard T Station**, orientate yourself in **Harvard Square ❶**, which is actually an amorphous area rather than a four-sided square. To the west lies the Coop, or Harvard Cooperative Society (a bookstore and department store founded in 1882). To the east **Harvard Yard** has the university's most historic buildings, bordered on the south and west by Massachusetts Avenue. The Yard is the geographic heart of America's oldest

and most prestigious university, founded in 1636. Six of Harvard's graduates have become US President, and it has churned out dozens of Nobel and Pulitzer prize-winners.

Enter Harvard Yard by the Johnston Gate, on the west arm of Massachusetts Avenue. To the right inside the gate is **Massachusetts Hall** (1718); look at its western gable to see the College Clock, painted in 18th-century style. To the left is **Harvard Hall**. This is the third version of the building, dating from 1766; the original, built in 1642, collapsed, and its 1682 replacement was razed by a fire in 1764. The inferno destroyed the largest library in the colonies, including John Harvard's own collection of books.

'The Statue of Three Lies'

Immediately ahead across the grass is **University Hall**, a white granite building designed by Charles Bulfinch in 1814. It now houses university offices, but was originally given over to dining rooms, classrooms, a chapel, and the president's office. The bronze statue of John Harvard in front of University Hall is nicknamed 'The Statue of Three Lies', because it is not of John Harvard, but of an 1884 undergraduate sculpted by Daniel French Chester; the inscription refers to John Harvard as founder of Harvard College, when he was in fact only the first major benefactor; and, contrary to the inscription, the college was not founded in 1638, the year of Harvard's bequest, but in 1636.

NEW YARD

Walk around University Hall into the Tercentenary Quadrangle, or **New Yard** ❷, which, on the first Monday of each June, is the scene of Commencement, Harvard's major graduation ceremony.

New Yard is dominated on the south by the **Widener Memorial Library** (closed to general public), with its grand Corinthian colonnade atop a monumental flight of stairs. Inside lie 56 miles (90km) of shelves, the third-largest library in the country and part of the largest university library in the world (13 million volumes). The Memorial Room, an elegant affair of wood paneling and stained-glass windows, contains Harry Widener's collection of rare books, including a Gutenberg Bible and a First Folio of Shakespeare.

Above from far left:
Memorial Hall;
students on the steps
of Widener Memorial
Library; colonnade.

The Swimming Test
The Widener Library is named after Harvard graduate Harry Elkins Widener, who drowned along with his father when the *Titanic* sunk. Legend has it that when his mother donated $2 million to found the library, it was on condition that all Harvard undergraduates pass a 50-yard swimming test. However, the test, no longer administered, predated Harry's attendance at Harvard.

Above from left:
Eliot House;
Mr Bartley's Burger
Cottage; butterflies in
the Museum of
Natural History;
Peabody Museum.

Below: Museum of
Natural History tiger;
campus tour.

Memorial Church and Sever Hall

The northern side of New Yard is punctuated by the soaring, delicate white spire of **Memorial Church**, which honors the Harvard dead in both world wars.

On the eastern side of the Yard is the Romanesque **Sever Hall**, considered one of architect H.H. Richardson's finest works. Its entrance is flanked by turreted towers, and the entire building is wonderfully rich in decorative brickwork.

ART MUSEUMS

Walk behind Sever Hall to emerge on Quincy Street, where you will find yourself facing the strikingly modern **Carpenter Center for the Visual Arts** ❸ (tel: 617-495-3251; www.ves.fas. harvard.edu; usually Mon–Sat 1–5pm; free), the only Le Corbusier building in North America. The ground-floor and third-floor galleries host exhibitions by international artists.

*Fogg Art Museum and
Busch-Reisinger Museum*

Next door at no. 32 are the **Fogg Art Museum** and **Busch-Reisinger Museum** ❹, both currently closed for renovations until 2013 *(see margin, opposite)*. The highlights of the Fogg include works by Ingres, and a fine collection of French Impressionist and Pre-Raphaelite works. In addition, there are dozens of Blake watercolors, and hundreds of Dürer and Rembrandt prints. The Busch-Reisinger collection, specializing in German art, includes 20th-century Expressionist canvases by Klee and Kandinsky, as well as the archives of architects Gropius and Feininger, forming the largest Bauhaus collection outside Germany.

Arthur M. Sackler Museum

During the renovations, pieces from both collections are being displayed in rotation at the nearby **Arthur M. Sackler Museum** ❺ (485 Broadway; tel: 617-495-9400; www.artmuseums. harvard.edu; Mon–Sat 10am–5pm, Sun 1–5pm; charge), alongside an outstanding collection of Chinese jades. The Sackler's Ancient and Islamic collections are also noteworthy.

Lunch Options

Either before or after visiting the Sackler, you can backtrack down Quincy Street to Massachusetts Avenue for lunch. Turn right to find **Mr Bartley's Burger Cottage**, see ⑪①, or walk further down the avenue toward Harvard Square and turn left on Dunster Street to arrive at **B.Good**, see ⑪②.

Harvard Tours

For the inside scoop on Harvard, take one of the student-led tours of the campus (Feb–Apr and mid-Sept–mid-Dec Mon–Fri 10am and 2pm, Sat 2pm, mid-June–mid-Aug Mon–Sat 10, 11.15am, 2 and 3.15pm; free), leaving from the Harvard University Information Center, Holyoke Center Arcade (1350 Massachusetts Avenue; tel: 617-495-1573; www.harvard.edu). A fun alternative is the 70-minute Unofficial Harvard Tour (tel: 617-848-8576; www.harv.unofficialtours.com; Sat–Sun 10.45am, 12.45 and 1.45pm; suggested donation $10), which leaves from Harvard Square outside Harvard T Station.

MEMORIAL HALL

Return to Quincy Street and follow it north across Cambridge Street. On the left is **Memorial Hall** ❻, a huge, red-brick Victorian Gothic pile, dating from 1874, with polychromatic roofs, which contains the Sanders Theater, the university's largest auditorium. Its somewhat truncated appearance is the result of a fire that destroyed the tall pinnacled roof over the central tower. If the building is open, pop in to admire the stained-glass windows.

On the right of Memorial Hall is the contrasting slender-pillared **Gund Hall**, built in 1969, and home of the Graduate School of Design.

PEABODY MUSEUM

Cross Kirkland Street and enter Divinity Avenue. This is flanked on the left side by the handsome, medieval-style **Adolphus Busch Hall** (named after the beer baron) and on the other by the William James Hall skyscraper, home to the Behavioral Science Department.

Toward the end of the avenue, on the left at no. 11, is the fascinating **Peabody Museum of Archaelogy and Ethnology** ❼ (tel: 617-495-7535; www.peabody.harvard.edu; daily 9am–5pm; charge). Among its superb collection of artifacts from around the globe are the only surviving Native American objects gathered by the explorers Meriwether Lewis and William Clark, who led the first American overland expedition to the Pacific coast (1804–6), as well as a huge photographic archive.

MUSEUM OF NATURAL HISTORY

Leaving the Peabody, turn right and right again to follow the footpath around the building to Oxford Street. Here, turn right once more to reach the entrance of the **Harvard Museum of Natural History** ❽ (tel: 617-495-3045; www.hmnh.harvard.edu; daily 9am–5pm; charge). Its most famous exhibit is the collection of over 3,000 extraordinarily lifelike handmade glass flowers. Kids will also love its collection of dinosaur remains, including a 12ft (3.5m) tall Plateosaurus.

TANNER FOUNTAIN

Exit back onto Oxford Street, and, turning left, continue past the Science Center, the largest building on Harvard campus. In front of it, amid a patch of grass to the north of Harvard Yard, stands the unusual **Tanner Fountain** ❾, gurgling amid a circular

New Art Museum

In 2008 the adjoining Fogg Art Museum and Busch-Reisinger Museum closed for major renovations. The plan is to bring the two art museums under the same roof as the Arthur M. Sackler Museum in a new building designed by Renzo Piano, slated to open in 2013. During the construction period the Sackler's galleries will be reconfigured to show key pieces from the collections of the Fogg and the Busch-Reisinger.

Food and Drink

① MR BARTLEY'S BURGER COTTAGE
1246 Massachusetts Avenue; tel: 617-354-6559; www.bartleys burgers.com; Mon–Sat 11am–9pm; $
A Harvard institution, this classic mom-and-pop burger joint offers a wide range of burgers named after famous politicians like Bill Clinton and Arnold Schwarzenegger ('this is no girly burger'). Wash them down with a raspberry lime rickey or a thick frappe.

② B.GOOD
24 Dunster Street; tel: 617-354-6500; www.bgood.com; Mon–Sat 11am–10pm, Sun 11am–9pm; $
Few restaurants can truly claim they serve healthy junk food, but B.Good actually does. Lean meats are hand-packed to create a variety of delicious burger combos, there are hand-cut baked fries and excellent salads. Eat in or take out.

grouping of 159 boulders – it's a lovely place to rest and take in the passing scene of students during term time.

Re-enter Harvard Yard. After passing Holworthy, Hollis, Stoughton, and Thayer – all freshman dormitories – you will be back by the Johnston Gate.

RADCLIFFE YARD

Cross Massachusetts Avenue and head west on Church Street. Just off to the left, on Palmer Street, is **Veggie Planet**, see ⑪③. Turn right at the junction with Brattle Street. Continue walking until you pass Appian Way. Next on the right is **Radcliffe Yard ⑩**, which is surrounded by a number of delightful late 19th- and early 20th-century buildings. This is where the renowned women's college of that name, now fully integrated with Harvard, began life in 1879.

Exit from the yard's far side onto Garden Street, which borders **Cambridge Common ⑪**. Surrounded by a semicircle of cannons, a bronze relief marks the spot where, on July 4, 1775, George Washington assumed command of the Continental Army.

LONGFELLOW HOUSE

Return through Radcliffe Yard to Brattle Street, and turn right to see why this is Cambridge's most prestigious street. Leafy and tranquil compared to busy Harvard Square, it is lined by splendid clapboard houses fronted by elegant porticoes, most from the 19th century, some from even earlier. Many bear blue plaques commemorating the great names who lived in them.

The most famous is the cream-colored clapboard building at no. 105, where Henry Wadsworth Longfellow composed many of his most famous works. It is now the **Longfellow National Historical Site ⑫** (tel: 617-876-4491; www.nps.gov/long; June–Oct Wed–Sun noon–4.30pm; charge). Even if the house *(see feature, right)* is closed, its pleasant grounds are always open for inspection.

Stroll back along Brattle Street toward Harvard Square, perhaps pausing at **L.A. Burdick Chocolate Shop and Café**, see ⑪④, or **The Red House**, see ⑪⑤, across Brattle Square on Winthrop Street.

Food and Drink 🍴

③ VEGGIE PLANET
Club Passim, 47 Palmer Street; tel: 617-661-1513; www.veggieplanet.net; Mon–Sat 11.30am–10.30pm, Sun 11am–10.30pm; $
A vegetarian restaurant with social responsibility. Didi Emmons lives up to her reputation as one of the most inventive vegetarian chefs in the city by creating tasty meatless pizzas and vegan meals. In the evening there's folk music.

④ L.A. BURDICK CHOCOLATE SHOP AND CAFÉ
52-D Brattle Street; tel: 617-491-4340; www.burdickchocolate.com; Mon–Thur 8am–9pm, Fri–Sat 8am–10pm, Sun 9am–9pm; $
A quiet oasis removed from the bustle of Harvard Square. Indulge in delectable handmade chocolates and pastries, accompanied by a great range of teas and coffees. Their hot chocolate is like dessert in a cup.

⑤ THE RED HOUSE
98 Winthrop Street; tel: 617-576-0605; www.theredhouse.com; Tue–Sun noon–midnight, Fri–Sat until 1am; $$
In a quaint red clapboard house, dating from 1802, this charming restaurant with a large outdoor deck serves most of its mains in half-portions – great if you are not so hungry or on a budget.

TOWARD THE CHARLES RIVER

From Winthrop Street turn right onto John F. Kennedy Street, and walk south past, on the left, the neo-Georgian **Kirkland House** ⓭ and **Eliot House**. Each residential co-ed house is a small college with about 400 students, and herein lies much of Harvard's strength: each house has its own administration and a veritable phalanx of tutors; its own library and dining hall; and its own exclusive societies and clubs. The concept was originally that of Edward Harkness, a Yale alumnus who, spurned by his alma mater, donated $13.8 million to Harvard in 1929 for the original seven houses.

On the other side of John F. Kennedy Street, facing Kirkland and Eliot houses, is Harvard's **John F. Kennedy School of Government** (www.hks. harvard.edu), fronted by the riverside John F. Kennedy Park.

Across busy Memorial Drive the handsome **Larz Anderson Bridge** ⓮, named in memory of Nicholas Longworth Anderson, a distinguished colonel in the US Civil War, spans the Charles River. From it there are superb views of the college, and, in the foreground, the Weld Boathouse, home of Harvard's women's crew. The boathouse to the right is home to the men's crew.

HARVARD BUSINESS SCHOOL

Cross the river, and continue straight on what is now North Harvard Street

for 100yds/m, passing on the right the Harvard playing fields and, on the left, the prestigious **Harvard Business School** ⓯. Turn left and stroll through the campus. Here the neo-Georgian buildings display a consistent rhythm of green doors, white window-frames, and red-brick walls.

Emerging on the school's eastern side, take the footbridge over busy Soldiers Field Road that leads to the **Weeks Memorial Footbridge** ⓰, which again offers an excellent view of some of Harvard's residential buildings.

Cross Memorial Drive and head north along DeWolfe Street aiming for Massachusetts Avenue, where a left turn will bring you back to Harvard Square.

Above from far left: graduation day; Weeks Memorial Footbridge; Harvard Business School.

Longfellow House History

When work started on the house in 1759 it stood amid 116 acres (47 ha) and was one of seven Tory estates occupying the area between Brattle Square and Elmwood Avenue. Abandoned by its owner John Vassal Jr in 1774, when patriots were making life difficult for loyalists in Cambridge, the house served as George Washington's headquarters for nine months during the siege of Boston. Longfellow took up residence as a lodger in 1837, received the house as a wedding gift from his father-in-law, and remained here until 1882.

CHARLES RIVER AND MIT

Experience both the relaxed and scientific side of Boston on this loop walk along the banks of the Charles River and through the campus of Massachusetts Institute of Technology (MIT), home to some of the nation's most innovative thinkers and eye-catching architecture.

DISTANCE 5½ miles (8.5km)

TIME A full day including museum visits

START/END Charles/MGH T Station

POINTS TO NOTE

If you plan to eat at 'The Trucks' on MIT campus, do this walk on a weekday. An early-morning tour of the Museum of Science is a good idea to avoid the crowds of schoolchildren that can descend on the place later in the day. MIT tours run throughout the year, but a visit during term time is recommended to experience the student atmosphere.

364.4 Smoots Plus One Ear

That's the length of the Harvard Bridge as measured using Oliver Reed Smoot, MIT class of 1962. For a prank his student buddies used the 5ft 7ins/1.7m Oliver as a yardstick. The paint squiggles counting off smoots along the bridge were retained when it was rebuilt in the 1980s.

Although the fast-moving traffic of Storrow Drive to the south and Memorial Drive to the north seems to isolate the Charles River from the city, pedestrian bridges over these highways mean that this riverside walk is easy to access. The route is popular with joggers, and, if you have a bicycle, it also makes for a very pleasant ride, with a dedicated cycle path most of the way. If you get tired, there are several points where you can exit the walk and hop back on the T.

You may wish to extend the walk along the river to connect with part of the Harvard route (see p.40).

LONGFELLOW BRIDGE

Exit Charles/MGH T Station on the Beacon Hill (southern) side and walk right toward the pedestrian bridge over Storrow Drive. On the other side turn right and head under the handsome **Longfellow Bridge**, often referred to as the Salt and Pepper Shaker Bridge, after the distinctive shape of its towers.

On the northern side of the bridge you will pass **Teddy Ebersol's Red Sox Fields ❶** (www.redsoxfoundation.org/ebersol), named after a young Red Sox fan who died in a plane crash. Here young athletes train in softball and soccer as well as baseball. Head past the kids' playground and the tennis courts to turn left from Storrow Drive onto the Charles River Dam. A metal grill here crosses the river at its narrowest point.

MUSEUM OF SCIENCE

Perched on Charles River Dam, with a life-sized model of a T rex outside, is the interactive and educational **Museum of Science** ❷ (tel: 617-723-2500; www.mos.org; Sat–Thur 9am–5pm, Fri 9am–9pm, July–Labor Day Sat–Thur 9am–9pm; charge). It takes several hours to do justice to the museum's 600-plus exhibits in six major fields:

astronomy, computing, energy, anthropology, industry, and nature.

Also here are the **Charles Hayden Planetarium** (separate charge), offering excellent programs on astronomy, plus laser light shows, and the **Mugar Omni Theater** (separate charge),

Above from far left: domed Maclaurin Building at MIT; Longfellow Bridge; exhibit at the Museum of Science.

World Rock Garden
As you leave the Museum of Science, take note of the small garden bordered by rock samples, some quite beautiful, from throughout the world, including pieces from the Grand Canyon, Giant's Causeway in Northern Ireland, and Mont Blanc.

Below: Museum of Science.

MIT Tours

Free student-led tours of MIT's campus run daily, at 11am and 3pm, from the information center in the lobby of 77 Massachusetts Avenue (tel: 617-253-4795).

where IMAX movies are projected onto a giant high-domed screen. Boston Duck Tours *(see margin, p.60)* depart from outside the museum.

EATING OPTIONS

Turn left on leaving the museum and, at the end of the bridge, turn left again onto Edwin H. Land Boulevard, which crosses the narrow Lechmere Canal. To the right is the large shopping mall **CambridgeSide Galleria** ❸ (www.cambridgesidegalleria.com), beyond which, on First Street, you can grab a snack at **Boca Grande**, see ⑪①. Alternatively, turn left onto Cambridge Parkway, passing the Charlesgate Yacht Club, to find **Dante**, see ⑪②, at the back of the Royal Sonesta Hotel.

Continue heading south along the river toward the Longfellow Bridge; the view here of the bridge with the city skyline behind is one of the best on the walk. Pass under the bridge and you will be walking alongside Memorial Drive. Cross this highway just after passing the Harvard Boat Club, walk down Wadsworth Street, and turn left on Amherst Street to enter the MIT campus. On the right at Carleton Street you will find **'The Trucks'**, see ⑪③.

MIT

Massachusetts Institute of Technology (MIT) was founded in 1861, and has been based here since 1916. Its reputation for science research obscures the fact that there is a fair amount of support for the arts on campus too.

List Visual Arts Center

Turn right at the end of Amherst Street to arrive at the **List Visual Arts Center** ❹ (Wiesner Building, 20 Ames Street; tel: 617-253-4444; http://web.met.edu/lvac; Tue–Sun noon–6pm, Thur until 8pm; free), which features temporary exhibits of superb contemporary art.

Ray and Maria Stata Center

Cross Ames Street and walk toward the whimsical **Ray and Maria Stata Center** ❺ (self-guided tour leaflet available from the information desk), a piece of Frank Gehry architecture that is a striking new addition to MIT.

MIT Museum

Exit the Stata Center on Vassar Street, head southwest to Massachusetts Avenue where you should hang a right to reach, at no. 265, the fascinating **MIT Museum** ❻ (tel: 617-253-4444; http://web.met.edu/museum; daily 10am–5pm; charge), which showcases the institute's history, scientific advances, and inventions, as well as the latter's artistic applications; check out the world's largest collection of holographic images. Part of the museum's collection is displayed back on the main campus in the **Hart Nautical Gallery** (55 Massachusetts Avenue; same hours; free).

MIT West Campus

Walk back along Massachusetts Avenue toward the river. Before entering the heart of MIT, through the grand portico on the left, take a moment to look at a couple of buildings on the western side of the campus.

Below: Simmons Hall dormitory has over 5,500 windows; Kresge Auditorium.

The **Kresge Auditorium** ➐ and the **MIT Chapel** facing it are two buildings designed by a Finnish architect, Eero Saarinen. The auditorium, completed in 1953, is an enormous tent-like structure rising out of a circular brick terrace. Two years later Saarinen designed the tiny multi-faith chapel, which is best appreciated from inside; there are no windows, but light floods in from the ceiling, bouncing off a hanging sculpture by Harry Bertola behind the altar.

MIT East Campus

From MIT's main entrance walk along the central hallway of the domed Maclaurin Building, known as 'The Infinite Corridor': weather permitting, the sun shines directly into the corridor twice a year. Exit the Maclaurin Building into grassy **Killian Court** ➑ facing the river. At the southern end is a sculpture by Henry Moore (right) and another by Michael Heizer (left).

HARVARD BRIDGE

Exit from the court and turn right along Memorial Drive. On the left is **Harvard Bridge** ➒ (also known as Massachusetts Avenue Bridge), the longest bridge across the Charles *(see margin, p.46)*, which provides sweeping views both up and down the river. At the bridge's end follow the footpath off to the left to reach the **Esplanade** ➓ (www.esplanadeassociation.org), a riverside park designed by Frederick Law Olmstead. The idyllic Storrow Lagoon, spanned by four small-arched stone bridges, extends for about a mile (nearly 2km).

BOSTON POPS

Beyond the lagoon is the **Hatch Shell** ⓫ (www.hatchshell.com), where free outdoor concerts, anchored by the Boston Pops Esplanade Orchestra, are held May to September. The highlight is the July 4 concert and fireworks display.

Behind the Shell is the boathouse of the Union Boat Club – the US's oldest rowing club, founded in 1851. Some 300yds/m beyond the boathouse is the clubhouse of **Community Boating** ⓬ (tel: 617-523-1038; www.community-boating.org), a public sailing program. Next to here is the footbridge back over the highway to Charles/MGH T Station.

Above from far left: Frank Gehry's Stata Center; students by the MIT Chapel; sailboats on the Charles.

Below: near the Hatch Shell is a bust of conductor Arthur Fiedler, who founded the Boston Sinfonietta in 1924, and went on to conduct its successor, the Pops.

Food and Drink

① BOCA GRANDE
149 First Street; tel: 617-354-5550; www.bocagrande.ypguides.net; Mon–Sat 10am–9pm; $
Rather than chowing down at the bland eateries in the CambridgeSide Galleria Mall, nip across the road to this kitsch, colorfully decorated café that serves dishes from Mexico's Oaxaca region.

② DANTE
Royal Sonesta Hotel, 40 Edwin H. Land Boulevard; tel: 617-497-4200; www.restaurantdante.com; Mon–Thur 6.30–10.30am, 11.30am–2.30pm, 5.30–10pm, Fri until 11pm, Sat 7am–2pm, 5.30–11pm, Sun 7am–2pm, 5–9pm; $$$
Dante's outdoor patio, overlooking the Charles River from the back of the Royal Sonesta Hotel, gives it unique appeal. That the three-Michelin-starred chef Dante de Magistris also turns out excellent Mediterranean-inspired cuisine is a bonus.

③ 'THE TRUCKS'
Carleton Street, MIT Campus; Mon–Fri 11am–3pm; $
Near the Kendall/MIT T Station, these food trucks are an MIT institution. Join throngs of students and alumni working in the area for lunch. There are four trucks, but the popular ones are always Goosebeary's for Chinese and Asian dishes, and José's Mexican.

BEACON HILL AND THE PUBLIC GARDEN

Packed with historic buildings, and the location of the Black Heritage Trail, Beacon Hill is one of Boston's most exclusive neighborhoods. A stroll here allows a glimpse into Boston's genteel past and elegant present.

DISTANCE 3 miles (5km)

TIME A half day

START Park Street T Station

END Arlington Street T Station

POINTS TO NOTE

If you want to tour the State House, do this walk on a weekday. You can easily extend the walk by browsing the many shops along Charles Street.

Below: ceiling detail from the State House.

The enchanting traffic-free streets of Beacon Hill are a delightful place to explore on foot. The most unswervingly traditional of all Boston's neighborhoods, the Hill has long been associated with wealthy 'Boston Brahmins' – the self-deprecating term coined by Oliver Wendell Holmes for the city's most illustrious families. However, Beacon Hill has always attracted a diverse population, with bohemian types residing on the north or 'bad' side – the derogatory term refers to the social standing of the residents rather than its contrast with the sunnier south side.

ROBERT GOULD SHAW MEMORIAL

This walk starts at **Park Street Station** at the northeastern corner of Boston Common. Head uphill through the park toward the Massachusetts State House. Immediately opposite this august institution pause to admire the **Robert Gould Shaw Memorial ❶**, honoring the first regiment of freed blacks in the Civil War. Their leader was 26-year-old white officer Robert Gould Shaw. The relief, sculpted by Augustus Saint Gaudens, depicts the regiment's farewell march down Beacon Street.

MASSACHUSETTS STATE HOUSE

At the crest of Beacon Street is the **Massachusetts State House ❷** (tel: 617-727-3676; www.sec.state.ma.us; Mon–Fri 10am–4pm; free), designed by Beacon Hill's pre-eminent architect Charles Bulfinch *(see p.12)* and completed in 1798. Dubbed 'the Hub of the Solar System' by Oliver Wendell Holmes, this regal building's most visually impressive feature, the glittering dome crowned in golf leaf in 1861, was originally covered with shingles.

Tour of the Interior
Take one of the 45-minute tours here to see the Doric Hall – a vaulted, columned marble hall with a statue of Washington – and the Hall of Flags, which displays the colors of state military units. A double stairway climbs to the chamber of the House of Representatives, an impressive oval room in which hangs the Sacred Cod, a gilded, carved-wood representation of the staple diet of the first settlers in the region and later a mainstay of both Boston's and the state's economy.

BOSTON ATHENAEUM

A short way further east down Beacon Street is the distinguished **Boston Athenaeum ❸** (tel: 617-227-0270; www.bostonathenaeum.org; Mon 8.30am–8pm, Tue–Sat 8.30am–5.30pm; free), a private library founded in 1807, about the same time the city was being touted as the 'Athens of America' for its cultural contributions to the nation. It is possible to visit the gallery here, but the library's half a million volumes – browsed by the likes of Ralph Waldo Emerson and Nathaniel Hawthorne – are off limits to all but members.

Backtrack to turn right on Bowdoin Street, where you will walk past the side of the State House to reach **Grotto**, see ⑪①, a fine lunch option.

OTIS HOUSE MUSEUM

Before heading into the heart of Beacon Hill, continue down Bowdoin Street until you reach Cambridge Street. A short distance to the left at no. 141 is the **Otis House Museum ❹** (tel: 617-227-3956; www.historicnewengland.org; Wed–Sun 11am–5pm; charge), the first of three homes in the area that Bulfinch designed in 1796 for Harrison Gray Otis, a real-estate developer turned politician. Today it is owned by the preservation body Historic New England, which has recreated the interior according to how it would have been at the turn of the 19th century.

> ### Food and Drink ⑪
> ① GROTTO
> 37 Bowdoin Street; tel: 617-227-3434; www.grottorestaurant.com; Mon–Fri 11.30am–3pm, 5–10pm, Sat–Sun 5–10pm; $$
> The basement location of this boho-chic Italian restaurant might be off-putting on a sunny day, but the food is well worth it. Salads, pastas, and sandwiches are all made with top-grade ingredients.

Above from far left: Beacon Hill facade; Otis House Museum interior; Massachusetts State House.

Statues at the State House
Since the State House gardens are off limits to the public, you will have to peer through the front railings to view these statues of famous Bostonians. From left to right they are: the religious martyr Anne Hutchinson, President John F. Kennedy *(pictured)*, educator Horace Mann, Civil War general Joseph Hooker, and another religious martyr, Mary Dyer.

Purple Glass

While strolling around Beacon Hill, look out for purple-glass window panes, such as at nos 40 and 39 Beacon Street. A cherished badge of age, the odd color is the result of excess manganese oxide in an early 19th-century shipment of glass from Europe that has darkened after years of exposure to sunlight.

Below: snapshots of the Museum of African American History.

NICHOLS HOUSE MUSEUM

Hike back up Hancock Street, turn right on Derne Street, then at the junction with Joy Street turn left and walk two blocks to Mount Vernon Street to enter the heart of the area. Here the tree-lined streets are narrower and bordered by elegant blocks of red-brick townhouses, enhanced by wrought-iron railings, window boxes of flowers, slender columns flanking doorways, delicate fanlights, and quirky brass door knockers.

Few of these homes are open to the public; one exception is the **Nichols House Museum** ❺ (55 Mount Vernon Street; tel: 617-227-6993; www.nicholshousemuseum.org; May–Oct Tue–Sat, Nov–Apr Thur–Sat noon–4pm; charge), well worth a visit. Inside this 1804 house, attributed to Bulfinch, is preserved the daily life of author and suffragette Ms Rose Standish Nichols, resident from 1885 to 1960.

PICTURESQUE STREETS

Turn left down Walnut Street, then right onto **Chestnut Street** where nos 13, 15, 17, and 29a provide further examples of Bulfinch's work; the latter is the oldest home on the South slope. Take the first right onto Willow Street and turn immediately left onto cobbled **Acorn Street**, one of Beacon Hill's most picturesque and most photographed streets. Acorn ends in West Cedar Street, where in the 1950s furious residents sat down

on the walkway to save the Hill's brick sidewalks from demolition. A right turn here leads back to Mount Vernon Street.

Mount Vernon Street

Henry James claimed **Mount Vernon Street** was 'the only respectable street in America.' Glancing up at no. 85, the free-standing **Second Harrison Gray Otis House** (1800), it is difficult to disagree. This Bulfinch building represents his vision of Mount Vernon Street, which he hoped would be lined by mansions, each in its own spacious grounds. Back at no. 88, fronting Louisburg Square, a plaque notes that the poet and Pulitzer Prize-winner Robert Lee Frost lived here from 1938 to 1941 while teaching at Harvard.

Louisburg Square

No such plaque commemorates Louisa May Alcott, who lived in **Louisburg Square** ❻ (the 's' is pronounced) at no. 10. Her literary success with *Little Women* allowed her to move here from the 'bad' side of the hill with her penniless parents and sisters.

The square's dignified red-brick row of houses, among the most expensive in Boston, includes, at the northeast corner, the home of former presidential candidate Senator John Kerry. In the centre is a small iron-fenced residents' park: an undistinguished statue of Columbus stands at the northern end, while at the southern end is one of Aristides the Just, a 5th-century BC Athenian statesman.

Pinckney Street

Exiting from the northern side of the square, turn right onto **Pinckney Street**, the dividing line between the posh South Slope and the less desirable North Slope. As well as aspiring writers, such as Louisa May Alcott, who lived at no. 20 with her family before she struck it rich, the street was home in the 19th century to a large and thriving African American community.

The red-brick condominium building at the corner of Anderson Street was once the **Phillips School 🗿**, which, when opened to African Americans in 1855, became the city's first interracial school. Across the street at no. 62 is one of several houses that were used as stopovers on the 'Underground Railroad' traveled by fugitive slaves on their way to freedom north of the border in Canada *(see feature, right)*.

At no. 24 is the aptly named **House of Odd Windows**, designed by a nephew of Ralph Waldo Emerson. Across the road, the delightful no. 9½ features an iron gate guarding a tunnel that passes through a house into a hidden courtyard surrounded by three other houses (not open to the public). No. 9, the small clapboard **Middleton-Glapion House**, dates from around 1795, making it one of the Hill's oldest properties.

MUSEUM OF AFRICAN AMERICAN HISTORY

Turn left onto Joy Street, walk downhill and you will arrive at Smith Court and the **Museum of African Ameri-** can History 🗿 (tel: 617-725-0022; www.afroammuseum.org; daily 10am–4pm; charge), housed in the Abiel Smith School, and dedicated in 1834 to the education of the city's African American children. Adjacent is the African Meeting House, the nation's oldest African American church. The museum's displays chart the contribution African Americans made to New England from colonial times through to the 19th century.

Anti-Slavery Meetings

At one time all the houses in Smith Court were occupied by African Americans. Also known as 'Black Faneuil Hall', the African Meeting House hosted anti-slavery meetings that culminated in 1832 with the founding of William Lloyd Garrison's New England Anti-Slavery Society.

Above from far left:
Acorn Street detail;
staircase in Nichols
House Museum;
Louisburg Square.

Underground Railroad

Beacon Hill was a key stop on the Underground Railroad, an informal network of secret routes and safe houses used by black slaves before the US Civil War to escape the southern US for the northern free states and Canada. Here the runaway slaves found many abolitionists and former slaves who were sympathetic to their cause.

You can find out more about the route while following the Black Heritage Trail. Starting at the Robert Gould Shaw Memorial and running through Beacon Hill, the trail explores the history of Boston's 19th-century African American community. Go to www.afroammuseum.org/trail.htm for a map and a self-guided tour of the trail's 14 sites or contact the National Park Service *(see p.104)* about its daily free guided tours.

Swanning Around

Ever since 1877, taking a turn on the Swan Boats (tel: 617-522-1966; www.swanboats.com; $2.75) on the lagoon of the Public Garden has been a fixture of the Boston scene. The paddle boats, which have been continuously operated by the Paget family, run from mid-April to mid-September, typically from 10am to 4pm.

Below: *Make Way for Ducklings* sculpture in the Public Garden; detail from the gates; colorful flowers.

Holmes Alley

Smith Court leads into narrow **Holmes Alley**, one of the 'secret' passageways along which fugitive slaves could escape from their pursuers *(see feature, p.53)* – follow its twists south then west to emerge on South Russell Street.

VILNA SHUL AND LEWIS HAYDEN HOUSE

At South Russell Street turn left, then right onto Myrtle Street, right again down Irving Street, and left onto Phillips Street. At no. 16 stands the **Vilna Shul ❾**, one of the area's last remaining synagogues, dating from 1919 but founded much earlier in a

---

Food and Drink 🍴

② CAFÉ VANILLE
70 Charles Street; tel: 617-523-9200; www.cafevanilleboston.com; Mon–Fri 6am–7pm, Sat–Sun 7am–7pm; $
Paris-trained bakers Bruno and Philip create mouthwatering cakes and pastries for sale alongside tasty sandwiches and coffee at this cute café, with outdoor tables in summer to enjoy Charles Street's passing parade.

③ PARAMOUNT CAFÉ
44 Charles Street; tel: 617-720-1152; www.paramountboston.com; Mon–Thur 7am–4.30pm, 5–10pm, Fri 7am–4.30pm, 5–11pm, Sat 8am–4.30pm, 5–11pm, Sun 8am–4.30pm, 5–10pm; $$
During the day it is an upscale diner with breakfast and lunch options aplenty. By night, it transforms into a candlelit café, with higher prices to match. A branch of the pizzeria Figs (see p.39) is a couple of doors down.

---

different location in the now demolished West End. The Boston area's largest Jewish community is now found to the west in the neighboring city of Brookline.

On the corner of Philips and Grove streets stands **Lewis Hayden House ❿**, a private residence that was one of most famous refuges for runaway slaves. The house was owned by Hayden, a former slave, who threatened to blow up anyone who dared try to search it – no one ever did.

Head south on Grove Street, and at Revere Street turn right and continue downhill to Charles Street, Beacon Hill's commercial hub.

CHARLES STREET

Lined with antiques shops, galleries, high-end specialty shops, and eateries, Charles Street is a pleasure to browse. A few hundred yards along on the left, next to **Café Vanille**, see ⑪②, is the former **Charles Street Meeting House ⑪**, now a complex of offices and stores. Recognizable by its lantern tower and clock, it was bought by the African Methodist Episcopalian Church in 1939. Further along, both the **Paramount Café**, see ⑪③, and **Figs** (at no.24; *see p.39*) are excellent dining options.

BEACON STREET

Turn left at the junction of Charles and Beacon streets. Facing Boston Common are some of the grandest Beacon Hill buildings. At **no. 50 ⑫**, on the corner of Spruce Street, a plaque commemorates Rev. Blackstone, the original Bostonian, who came to live at this spot – then known as Shawmut by the Native Americans – in 1625.

The Federal-style building at **no. 45** is the third house built by Bulfinch for Harrison Gray Otis, who lived here from 1806 until his death in 1848. It is now occupied by the American Meteorological Society (tel: 617-227-2426; www.ametsoc.org; free), and if you call in advance it is sometimes possible to arrange tours of its interior.

Almost next door, at **no. 42**, the glistening white granite building with two large bow windows belongs to the exclusive Somerset Club. The attitude of this establishment's members can be seen from the time the club caught fire, and firefighters were told to use the tradesmen's entrance – marked by a handsome pair of lion doorhandles.

THE PUBLIC GARDEN

Retrace your steps back downhill to the corner of Charles and Beacon streets, where you can enter the glorious **Public Garden**, the oldest botanical garden in the US. Although not large, it has magnificently maintained formal flower beds and a lovely lagoon, bordered by weeping willows, on which float the famous Swan Boats *(see margin, left)*.

Make Way for Ducklings
Close by the Charles Street entrance is the charming *Make Way for Duck-*

lings sculpture ⑬, based on the characters in the classic American children's book of the same name by Robert McCloskey (first published in 1941) – it is always a hit with the little ones.

Head from here toward the miniature suspension bridge over the lagoon. Ahead you will see a splendid equestrian **statue of Washington** ⑭. The first president was also, according to Jefferson, the finest horseman of the age.

Emerge from the garden here at the foot of Commonwealth Avenue where you can start walk 6 *(see p.56)*, or you can continue south to the corner of Arlington and Boylston streets, where you will find the Arlington T stop.

(see p.56)

Above from far left: Swan Boats and flowers in the Public Garden.

Below: statue of Washington.

BACK BAY

Back Bay, with its neat grid pattern and alphabetical progression of the cross streets from Arlington to Hereford, is bisected by the grand boulevard of Commonwealth Avenue. Around it there are historic mansions and churches, and the choice shopping precincts of Newbury Street and Copley Place.

DISTANCE 3½ miles (5.5km)
TIME A half day
START Arlington T Station
END Symphony T Station
POINTS TO NOTE

You may wish to allow time to browse Back Bay's many shops. If you do the walk after lunch, you could end with a sunset drink at the Top of the Hub.

Originally a shallow estuary, Back Bay was filled in and laid out by mid-Victorian believers in the urban grid pattern, eager to make expansive use of 'made land' and put Downtown's tortuous alleys and the narrow streets of Beacon Hill behind them. This was Boston's most exclusive address until the Great Depression of the 1930s saw aristocratic homes converted into apartments and college dormitories. It has now regained its former glory, and is home to Boston's new wealth.

COMMONWEALTH AVENUE

From Arlington T Station walk north on Arlington Street, passing the brownstone **Arlington Street Church ❶**, considered to be the 'mother church' of Unitarianism in the US, and one of first buildings to rise in Back Bay in 1861. Continue past the east end of Newbury Street – there will be a chance to trawl its boutiques later – and the Taj Boston (formerly the Ritz-Carlton and still something of an institution; *see p.111*).

The next corner leads to the foot of **Commonwealth Avenue**, Back Bay's pièce de résistance. Commonly known as Com Ave, this French-inspired boulevard has a 100ft (30m) wide strip of park adorned by statues running down its middle. Magnificent buildings, many once single family homes, line either side of the street. For a glimpse inside one, call in at no. 5, the **Boston Center for Adult Education** ❷ (tel: 617-247-3606; www.bcae.org; Mon–Fri 9am–5pm; free). Built in 1904 for Walter C. Baylies, the mansion includes a grand ballroom, reminiscent of the Petit Trianon at Versailles, that the textile industrialist added on for his daughter's coming-out party.

BEACON STREET

Gibson House Museum

Turn right on Berkeley Street, walk to the corner of Beacon Street, and turn right again to arrive at no. 137, the **Gibson House Museum** ❸ (tel: 617-267-6338; www.thegibsonhouse.org; tours Wed–Sun 1, 2 and 3pm; charge). This 1860 Italian Renaissance-style row house from the first period of Back Bay construction comes complete with original Victorian furnishings, preserved intact through the tenure of the last owner, a scion of the Gibson family who died in the 1950s.

Isabella Stewart Gardner

Continue west along Beacon Street, where on the right side you will pass **no. 150**, a splendid Italian Renaissance Revival building that was the home of Isabella Stewart Gardner, Boston's most famous private art collector, before she moved to the Fenway *(see p.66)*. Mrs Gardner actually lived at no. 152, but when she moved the eccentric heiress insisted that the

number never be used again on the street. Her wish has been respected.

Goethe Institute

A little further along, at no. 170, it is possible to look inside the **Goethe Institute** ❹ (tel: 617-262-6050; www. goethe.de/boston; Mon–Fri 9am–5pm; free), a German cultural center based in a 1901 home, with a beautifully preserved frieze in its library and a view across the Charles River.

BACK ON COMMONWEALTH AVENUE

From the Goethe Institute turn left onto Clarendon Street and return to Commonwealth Avenue, where you will note the **First Baptist Church** ❺, dating from the early 1870s, and affectionately known as the 'Church of the Holy Bean Blowers' after the trumpeting angels at the corners of its tower. The faces of the frieze (modeled by Auguste Batholdi, sculptor of the Statue of Liberty) that decorate the top of the church's tower are said to be likenesses of notable Bostonians, such as Longfellow, Emerson, and Hawthorne.

Notable Mansions

Continue down the spine of Commonwealth Avenue to the intersection with Dartmouth Street. The grand corner building on the right-hand side is the **Ames-Webster Mansion** ❻ (306 Dartmouth Street), dating from 1872. Much of its elaborate interior design, including a grand hall with carved-oak panels, 18ft (5½m) high

Firefighters' Memorial
Among the many sculptures dotted along Commonwealth Avenue's central boulevard, one of the most poignant is at the intersection with Clarendon Street – it is the memorial to the nine firemen who died fighting the blaze at the Hotel Vendôme (160 Commonwealth Avenue) in 1973.

Above from left:
Trinity Church apse;
Bates Hall reading
room in Boston
Public Library.

Below: library lion.

ceilings, and stained-glass windows, was preserved when the building was turned into commercial offices later in its life.

Head further down the avenue to the intersection with Hereford Street. On the right is **John F. Andrews House** ❼ (32 Hereford Street), Back Bay's first Italian Renaissance Revival-style building, now well maintained by an MIT fraternity. On the opposite side, at 314 Commonwealth Avenue, ornamentation runs riot at the flamboyant **Burrage House** ❽, built in 1899, a synthesis of Vanderbilt-style mansion and French chateau.

SHOPPING ON NEWBURY STREET

Turn left off Commonwealth Avenue at Massachusetts Avenue and walk a block to **Newbury Street**, Back Bay's most eclectic shopping destination. At this end of Newbury the vibe is studenty and hip, as typified by the clientele of **The Other Side Café**, see ⑪①, and **Trident Booksellers and Café**, see ⑪②, next door to which you will find Newbury Comics (www.new burycomics.com), one of Boston's best music, video, and comics stores.

Further down Newbury you can browse antiques stores and art galleries, and there are lots of appealing cafés and restaurants, some with street-side dining in the warmer months; a classic option is **Stephanie's on Newbury**, see ⑪③. The closer you get to Arlington Street the more upmarket the stores become, featuring the likes of Giorgio Armani, Brookes Brothers, and Loro Piana. The chic boutique department store **Louis Boston** ❾, on the corner of Newbury and Berkeley streets, occupies an 1862 manse that was once the Museum of Natural History.

COPLEY SQUARE

From Louis Boston you could turn left onto busy Boylston Street, where you will soon hit the **Parish Café**, see ⑪④,

Food and Drink

① THE OTHER SIDE CAFÉ
407 Newbury Street; tel: 617-536-8437; Mon–Thur 9am–midnight, Fri–Sat 9am–1am, Sun 10am–midnight; $
A hipster hangout with a vegetarian-friendly menu and a nice selection of specialty coffees and beers on tap as well as organic, biodynamic wines. The front patio is a popular place to have drinks or brunch.

② TRIDENT BOOKSELLERS AND CAFÉ
338 Newbury Street; tel: 617-267-8688; www.tridentbooks cafe.com; Mon–Sun 9am–midnight; $
A hold-over from the hippie era where you can buy a coffee and nurse it all day without being rushed out. Its simple fare, such as homemade soups, fresh salads, and daily specials, draws a loyal clientele.

③ STEPHANIE'S ON NEWBURY
190 Newbury Street; tel: 617-236-0990; www.stephanieson newbury.com; Mon–Sat 11.30am–11pm, Sun 10am–10pm; $$
Stephanie's large outdoor patio is the place to see and be seen while dining on Newbury Street. The salads are the stars, but the rest of the menu is tasty too. In chillier weather enjoy a drink by the side of the roaring fireplace.

④ PARISH CAFÉ
361 Boylston Street; tel: 617-247-4777; www.parishcafe.com; Mon–Sat 11.30am–1am, Sun noon–1am; $$
The menu of sandwiches designed by some of Boston's celebrity chefs is a little gimmicky but it nevertheless works. There is an extensive list of beers and other drinks, and the outdoor patio in the summer complements the experience.

and Arlington T Station, a possible exit point from this walk if you are feeling tired. However, Back Bay still has plenty more to offer, so, if you wish to continue, turn right instead at Boylston and walk a block to reach **Copley Square ⑩**, named after the great Boston painter John Singleton Copley and one of the city's focal points.

Trinity Church

Copley Square's most renowned building, on the eastern side, is **Trinity Church** (tel: 617-536-0944; www. trinitychurchboston; Tue–Sat 9am–5.30pm, Sun 1–5pm; charge), a seminal work in American architecture that initiated the Romanesque revival. Enter through the west porch, which leads into a richly decorated interior. The superb frescoes are the work of John La Farge, who also supervised the stained-glass windows.

Rising up 62 stories behind the church is the I.M. Pei-designed **John Hancock Tower**, with 10,000 panels of mirrored glass reflecting all around it.

Boston Public Library

Facing the western side of Copley Square is the venerable **Boston Public Library ⑪** (tel: 617-536-5400; www. bpl.org; Mon–Thur 9am–9pm, Fri–Sat 9am–5pm, Oct–May also Sun 1–5pm; free), designed by Charles Follen McKim in 1852. The interior of the old wing is spectacular. Climb a grand stairway to the second floor to view one of the library's murals, a painting of the Nine Muses by the Parisian artist Puvis de Chavannes.

On the right is **Bates Hall**, an enormous reading room with a barrel-vaulted ceiling, named after Joshua Bates, the library's first major benefactor. An adjoining room displays Pre-Raphaelite murals of the Quest for the Holy Grail.

Go up one more floor to see the **John Singer Sargent Gallery**, featuring a series of powerful murals on religious themes.

The lovely Italian-cloistered **courtyard** in the center of the building is

Library Tours

There are often fine-art and photography exhibitions in the Boston Public Library. Free art and architecture tours depart from Dartmouth Street lobby in the old wing (Mon 2.30pm, Tue and Thur 6pm, Fri and Sat 11am, Sun 2pm).

Below: Trinity Church and John Hancock Tower.

Above from left:
Christian Science Plaza and, to the left, the Prudential Center; Top of the Hub restaurant; New Old South Church.

one of the city's most peaceful retreats, and you can enjoy it with refreshments from **Novel**, see ⑪⑤.

New Old South Church

Opposite the Public Library on the corner of Bolyston and Dartmouth streets is the striking Italian Gothic campanile of the **New Old South Church ⑫**, dating from 1875; the original Old South still stands Downtown and can be visited on walk 1 *(see p.29)*. The church's original 246ft (75m) tower, which began to lean soon after construction, had to be dismantled and rebuilt slightly lower in 1931.

Duck Tours
Departing from Huntington Avenue, between Copley Place and the Prudential Center, are the popular Duck Tours (tel: 617-723-3825; www.bostonduck tours.com; Apr–Nov 9am–dusk; $26), which use amphibious vehicles built in World War II (nicknamed 'ducks') for the 90-minute narrated land and water circuit around Boston. The same tour can also be joined outside the Museum of Science *(see pp.46–7)*; advance booking is advised.

Food and Drink 🍴

⑤ NOVEL
Boston Public Library, 700 Boylston Street; tel: 617-385-5660; www.bpl.org; Mon–Fri 11.30am–2pm, 2.30–4pm; $
Serves an elaborate lunch buffet with homemade soups, hot and cold entrees, and luscious desserts, as well as a set afternoon tea later in the day – all with a view of the library courtyard's fountain. Next door the self-serve Map Room Café is open Mon–Sat 9am–5pm.

⑥ TOP OF THE HUB
52nd floor, Prudential Tower; tel: 617-536-1775; www.topofthe hub.net; Mon–Sat 11.30am–1am, Sun 11am–1am; $$$
The food is generally overpriced, but this is a romantic place with a phenomenal view for drinks and nibbles at sundown. After 8pm there is a $24 minimum spend but also live jazz. Advance reservation is recommended.

COPLEY PLACE

Head in the other direction toward where Huntington Avenue meets Darmouth Street at the entrance to the Westin Hotel, which is part of **Copley Place ⑬**, central Boston's largest and glitziest shopping and office complex. Follow the corridors through the building to arrive at two floors of upmarket stores surrounding a nine-story atrium, in the center of which is a 60ft (18m) travertine and granite waterfall sculpture.

PRUDENTIAL CENTER

An enclosed walkway from Copley Mall leads you over Huntington Avenue into the **Prudential Center**, another shopping mall surrounding the 52-story Prudential Tower. On the 50th floor is the **Skywalk ⑭** (tel: 617-859-0648; www.topofthehub.net; daily 10am–10pm; charge), which provides 360-degree views of the city through floor-to-ceiling windows, as well as the *Dreams of Freedom* exhibition about the history of immigration in Boston. This is an ideal spot to return to at the end of the walk to enjoy a cocktail at the **Top of the Hub**, see ⑪⑥, the restaurant and bar on the tower's 52nd floor.

Unless you hire a helicopter to fly over the city, the bird's-eye views from either of Prudential's venues are pretty exceptional; the viewing gallery at the top of the nearby John Hancock Tower, for example, closed after 9/11.

CHRISTIAN SCIENCE PLAZA

Exit the Prudential Center at the corner of Huntington Avenue and Belvidere Street, across from which lies the 670ft (200m) long reflecting pool that forms the centerpiece of the **Christian Science Plaza** ⓖ, designed by I.M. Pei in the early 1970s and one of the most monumental public spaces in the city.

Christian Science Church

Along the north side of pool runs the five-story Colonnade Building, culminating in the separate **Christian Science Church** ⓰ (tel: 617-450-3790; www.tfccs.com; Tue noon–4pm, Wed 1–4pm, Thur–Sat noon–5pm, Sun 11am–3pm; free), the original church of the movement founded by Mary Baker Eddy (1821–1910) and headquartered in Boston since 1882.

The church is entered through a dramatic basilica-like structure, a mixture of Byzantine and Italian Renaissance styles. As you will discover on the guided tour, this part is the church's 1906 extension that seats 3,000 on three levels. The pipe organ here is one of the largest in the Western hemisphere.

Tucked behind this is the original Mother Church from 1894, with 82 beautiful stained-glass windows depicting biblical events.

Mary Baker Eddy Library and Mapparium

On leaving the church, immediately to the right, with its entrance at 200 Massachusetts Avenue, is the **Mary Baker Eddy Library and Mapparium** ⓱ (tel: 617-450-7000; www.marybakereddylibrary.org; Tue–Sun 10am–4pm; charge). The highlight of the beautifully designed interior is the Mapparium (last show at 3.40pm), a globe 30ft (9m) in diameter, made up of 608 stained-glass panels, and into which you can walk. It provides a snapshot of the world as it was in 1935. The echoing acoustics are uncanny.

Exit from the library onto Massachusetts Avenue. Head southeast along the road and you will eventually come to Symphony T Station.

Sneaker Shop
Around the corner from the Mary Baker Library at 6 Clearway is the unmarked store Bodega (www.bdga store.com). From the outside it may look like an old convenience store, but stand in front of its drink-vending machine to open the secret door into an ultra-cool sneaker and street-wear boutique.

Below: Christian Science Church.

BACK BAY FENS

Beyond Massachusetts Avenue, architecturally dense Back Bay yields to the Fenway, a loose scattering of institutions and apartment buildings joined by the meandering path of the Back Bay Fens, an urban archipelago of parkland.

Red Sox Tickets
The Red Sox are so popular that tickets for a game are snapped up as swiftly as they go on sale. Check the Red Sox website for what's available, or turn up early (real early) on match day for standing-room-only tickets, sold from the Gate C ticket window.

DISTANCE 1¼ miles (2km)
TIME 2 hours
START Kenmore T Station
END Longwood Medical Area T Station
POINTS TO NOTE

This walk can be combined with tour 8 covering the Museum of Fine Arts and the Isabella Stewart Gardner Museum. The area around Victory Gardens in the Fens is a notorious gay cruising area and site of muggings, so bear in mind that it is not safe to explore at night.

Food and Drink

① UBURGER
636 Beacon Street; tel: 617-536-0448; www.uburgerboston.com; Mon–Sat 11am–11pm, Sun noon–11pm; $
This generic-looking café is the new Mecca of Boston burger-lovers. They grind their own prime beef, hand-cut their fries and onion rings, and charge just $4 for their burgers. At lunch the line can be out the door.

② LA VERDAD TAQUERIA
1 Lansdowne Street; tel: 617-421-9595/617-351-2580; www.laverdadtaqueria.com; counter: Tue–Thur 11am–1am, Fri–Sat 11am–2am; restaurant: Tue–Thur 5pm–1am, Fri 5pm–2am, Sat 11am–2am; $–$$
At the end of Boston's main nightclub strip, chef Ken Oringer's latest venture, specializing in Mexican street food, is a sharp departure from his gourmet restaurant Clio (in the Eliot Suite Hotel; *see p.111*). Tortillas are made on premises and sauces from scratch. The *carne asada* soft tortilla is excellent.

KENMORE SQUARE

Begin at **Kenmore Square ❶**, where Commonwealth Avenue, Brookline Avenue, and Beacon Street meet beneath the gaze of the giant Citgo sign. If you arrive by the T, take the Fenway exit to emerge on the southern side of Commonwealth Avenue. On the northern side of the Square, where you will find **Uburger**, see ⑪①, and further west along Commonwealth Avenue lies the sprawling campus of Boston University.

FENWAY PARK

Hang a left into Brookline Avenue and head over the Massachusetts Turnpike for a view of the back of the Green Monster. This is the nickname of the left field wall of **Fenway Park ❷** (tel: 617-236-6666; www.redsox.com; tours in season: 9am–4pm or 3½ hours prior to game time, off-season: 9am–3pm; charge), home to the Red Sox baseball team.

Built in 1912, Fenway Park is the smallest and oldest stadium in the major leagues. Baseball legends like Ted Williams and Carl Yastrzemski played their entire careers here. Red Sox fans, heartbroken since 1918, the last year Boston won a World Series, rejoiced when the team brought home the trophy in 2004 and again in 2007. Tours of the ground allow you to peer into the press box and down from the Monster.

Walking around the ground's perimeter, turn left into Yawkey Way where you will find the official store for Red Sox souvenirs. Turn left at Van Ness Street and walk along the ball park's southern side to encounter a statue of **Ted Williams ❸** beside Gate B. You could continue down Ipswich Street to grab a snack at **La Verdad Taqueria**, see ⑪②. Turning right from Ted's statue will quickly bring you to Bolyston Street across which are the Back Bay Fens.

BACK BAY FENS

The reedy marshland along the Muddy River (a creek, actually) is a major link in the Emerald Necklace – nine green spaces designed by Frederick Law Olmsted, also responsible for New York's Central Park. Immediately across Park Drive from Boylston Street are the **Fenway Victory Gardens ❹** (www.fenwayvictorygardens.com; free), a 7-acre (3 ha) allotment site created in 1942. There are some charmingly crafted small gardens here with flower beds, rockeries, and pergolas. Further around the Fens, just south from Agassiz Road, is the more formal **James P. Kelleher Rose Garden ❺**, established in 1930.

ART SCHOOLS

A footbridge at the southern end of the Fens will take you across the creek to the Fenway entrance of the **Museum of Fine Arts** *(see p.64)*. Next to it, on the corner of Museum Road and Evans

Way, is the **School of the Museum of Fine Arts ❻** (tel: 617-369-3718; www.smfa.edu; free), which hosts exhibitions by students and up-and-coming artists. Outside stands Katherine Lane Weerns' regal bronze statue *Rhinoceros*.

More contemporary art can be seen in the galleries of nearby **Massart ❼** (621 Huntington Avenue; tel: 617-879-7333; www.massart.edu; free), the Massachusetts College of Art, just southwest across Evans Way. Hop back on the T at Longwood Medical Area Station.

Above from far left: the Citgo Sign, an unlikely emblem of Boston, has lorded it over Kenmore Square since 1965; baseball at Fenway Park; Red Sox fan.

8 TWO ART MUSEUMS

While the Museum of Fine Arts boldly strides into the future with its new wing and renovations, time stands still at the Isabella Stewart Gardner Museum. A day spent exploring these two wonderful collections will take you from Egyptian antiquities to masterpieces of 20th-century art.

Evening Entertainment

As well as evening gallery viewings in the MFA from Wednesday to Friday, there is a highbrow selection of world cinema screened in the MFA's Remis Auditorium, while live music is held in the Calderwood Courtyard in summer (see www.mfa.org). The Isabella Stewart Gardner Museum stays open until 9pm on the third Thursday of the month.

DISTANCE ¼ mile (0.5km)
TIME A full day
START/END Museum of Fine Arts T Station
POINTS TO NOTE
The distance above covers the short walk between the two museums. An evening visit to the MFA is possible Wednesday to Friday, but only on Wednesday are all the galleries open until 9.45pm.

Such are the treasures contained inside these two museums that you should set aside a day for them – to spend anything less would be doing the wonderful collections a disservice. The Museum of Fine Arts T stop makes getting here and away a breeze, although if you are quick getting around the museums, you can

easily add on walk 7 *(see p.62)* to stretch your legs further across the Back Bay Fens. The hardest decision all day is likely to be choosing in which of the institutions' excellent cafés to have lunch.

MUSEUM OF FINE ARTS

Ranked second only to New York's Metropolitan among American museums, the **Museum of Fine Arts ❶** (MFA; 465 Huntington Avenue; tel: 617-267-9300; www.mfa.org; Sat–Tue 10am–4.45pm, Wed–Fri 10am–9.45pm; charge) first opened in 1870. It moved into the present building, designed by Guy Lowell, in 1909, and is currently getting a major facelift *(see feature, right)*.

The highly cultured citizens of 19th-century Boston were keen collectors, amassing art and antiquities from around the world. Their bequests have resulted in the MFA not only having one of the foremost holdings outside Paris of Impressionist painting (in particular works by Monet, Pissarro, Sisley, Renoir, and Manet), but also an outstanding collection of Japanese art. The American art collection is one of the best in the US; the European and American decorative arts rooms display superb silver, porcelain, furniture, and musical instruments. The Nubian and Egyptian collections are practically unrivaled too.

Planning Your Visit

There is so much to see here – and there will be even more come 2010 – that time-pressed visitors are well advised either to pick out just one collection, or take one of the (free) guided tours that highlight the best from all the collections.

Approach the MFA from the T Station, and enter at the Huntington Street entrance, outside of which Cyrus Edwin Dallin's bronze equestrian statue *Appeal to the Great Spirit* has stood since 1913.

American Art

The MFA's excellent collection of American art is the main draw on the lower-floor galleries accessed off the lower rotunda. The new galleries for the **Art of the Americas** will be off to the right *(see feature, below)*.

Among the works to look out for are portraits by John Singleton Copley, Gilbert Stuart (including the one of George Washington that was the source of the design on the dollar bill), and John Singer Sargent: his *The Daughters of Edward Darley Boit* is a particularly striking composition, and he painted the spectacular murals of scenes from Greek mythology around the **Upper Rotunda** in the centre of the MFA.

Other highlights include paintings from the mid-19th century Hudson River School and those of Edward Hopper from the 20th century. There is also a fine collection of American decorative arts, including silver made by Paul Revere.

Above from far left: Museum of Fine Arts and Cyrus Edwin Dallin's sculpture *Appeal to the Great Spirit*; gallery of Renaissance art; Edward Hopper's *Lighthouse and Buildings, Portland Head, Cape Elizabeth* (1927).

Below left: Renoir's *Dance at Bougival* (1883).

The New MFA

By late 2010 a new chapter in the Museum of Fine Arts' history will be revealed. This is when the Sir Norman Foster-designed four-level wing for the Art of the Americas is slated to open, making the MFA around 28 per cent larger. As part of this major renovation, the first since I.M. Pei's West Wing was added in 1981, the grand Fenway Entrance, facing onto the Fenway, has been reinstated. Next door you will find the new Sharf Visitor Center. The European galleries are also being updated; the West Wing will be devoted entirely to contemporary art; and there will be a new public space, the Glass Courtyard, linking the galleries of the new wing to the rest of the museum. With so many changes ahead, check with the Sharf Visitor Center for the exact location of the art that you wish to see.

MFA Cafés

Apart from its Bravo restaurant, the MFA also offers the Galleria Café next to the bookshop, serving light snacks and drinks, and the self-service Courtyard Café with seating in summer out in the Calderwood Courtyard. Both are open daily 10am–4pm.

Egyptian Treasures

For 40 years from 1905, Harvard University and the Museum of Fine Arts collaborated on an archeological excavation in Egypt, based at the Great Pyramids at Giza. From this the museum acquired a world-famous collection of **Egyptian antiquities**, located in the galleries to the right of the Upper Rotunda on the second floor. Among many Old Kingdom sculptures is a beautiful statue of King Mycerinus, who built the Third Pyramid at Giza, and his queen, dated to around 2548–2530BC. Other treasures include gilded and painted mummy masks, and some remarkably well-preserved hieroglyphic inscriptions.

The Giza expedition's director, Dr George A. Reisner, also worked in the Sudan, and brought home a dazzling collection of Nubian artifacts, the best in the world outside Khartoum. Particularly awe-inspiring are the exquisite gold jewelry, inlaid with enamel and precious stones, and sculptures, varying in size from huge statues of Nubian kings to tiny funerary figurines.

Asian Art

Visitors to the MFA are frequently astonished to find it has one of the largest collection of Japanese art outside Japan, spread over two floors of **Japanese Galleries** in the museum's southwestern section. The highlight is a temple-like room displaying six massive Buddhas; but take time also to view the intricate beauty of the displayed woodblock prints, textiles, and painted silk screens.

A lovely place to collect your thoughts is the tranquil Japanese-style walled garden **Tenshin-En**, the Garden of the Heart of Heaven. It was designed by Kyoto artist Kinsaku Nakane to suggest the landscape of New England. Located in the MFA's western corner, the garden is open mid-April through mid-October, 10am to 4pm, weather permitting. On the way to the garden you will pass the stairs and elevators up to **Bravo**, see ⑪①.

ISABELLA STEWART GARDNER MUSEUM

Exit the MFA via its West Wing onto Museum Road. Turn right and at the end of the road turn left. On reaching Evans Way cross the small strip of parkland to find the magical **Isabella Stewart Gardner Museum ❷** (tel: 617-566-1401; www.gardnermuseum. org; Tue–Sun 11am–4.45pm; charge).

Food and Drink 🍴

① BRAVO

Museum of Fine Arts, 465 Huntington Avenue; tel: 617-369-3474; daily 11.30am–3pm, Wed–Fri 5.30–8.30pm; $$$
The MFA's fine-dining restaurant is a delightfully relaxed space in which to enjoy lunch or dinner (when there is live piano music). Wine-tastings are held the last Wednesday of the month from 5.30–7.30pm, and jazz is played at Sunday brunch.

② GARDNER CAFÉ

Isabella Stewart Gardner Museum, 280 Fenway; tel: 617-566-1088; Tue–Fri 11.30am–4pm, Sat–Sun 11am–4pm; $$
You can eat at the Gardner Café without paying to visit the attached museum, although it would be a shame to come here just for the food. The seasonal menu is delicious enough to throw local reviewers into fits of ecstasy, particularly over the scrumptious bread pudding.

Fenway Court, the Venetian-style palazzo that houses the museum, was built in 1902 by heiress Isabella Stewart (1840–1924), an eccentric New Yorker who married Jack Lowell Gardner. She scandalized Boston society by drinking beer rather than tea, and walking her pet lions in the Back Bay. Her portrait by John Singer Sargent reveals what was then considered a daring décolletage, but on seeing the notorious picture here at Fenway Court (it hangs in the Gothic Room on the third floor), you might well wonder what all the fuss was about.

Mrs Gardner's Will

The renowned art historian Bernard Berenson advised Mrs Gardner on acquisitions, but their presentation and positioning is the result of her inimitable approach. Each room is decorated in a different style, although none is true to any specific period. Mrs Gardner died in 1924, and her will stipulated that everything in the museum remain exactly as she arranged it; otherwise the building and its contents were to be sold and the proceeds given to Harvard University. Were it not for this legal embalmment, a good part of her collection could have been consigned to the storeroom – an unfortunate fate for priceless works by Giotto and Piero della Francesca.

Collection and Courtyard

Among the eclectic collection you will see Dutch baroque and Italian Renaissance masterpieces, Titians and Rembrandts, Whistlers and Sargents, Matisses and Manets, stained glass and textiles.

Even those impervious to the aesthetic qualities of such art are sure to delight in the **central courtyard**. Many of its elements were imported from Venice, and it is ablaze with flowers throughout the year. To sit here, far from the madding crowd, is sheer bliss. So too are the **chamber music concerts** in the tapestry room on the second floor (late Sept–early May Sun 1.30pm).

For refreshments head to the **Gardner Café**, see ⓵②. During the summer months seats from the café flow outside into the adjoining Monks Gardens.

Above from far left: Japanese-style garden Tenshin-En; Upper Rotunda; the MFA features an impressive collection of Egyptian treasures; courtyard of the Isabella Stewart Gardner Museum.

Left: John Singer Sargeant's 'daring' portrait of Isabella Stewart Gardner.

THE SOUTH END

Few Boston neighborhoods have gone on such a roller-coaster ride of respectability and real-estate values as the South End. Today it is a magnet for artists, trendy singletons, and young families, all attracted by the area's architecture, shops, galleries, and restaurants.

DISTANCE 2¾ miles (4.5km)
TIME A half day
START/END Back Bay/South End T Station
POINTS TO NOTE
Do this walk in the morning, so you can have breakfast at Charlie's Sandwich Shoppe. You may wish to extend the time taken to walk the route by browsing the South End's many shops and galleries.

The South End, immediately south of Back Bay, is delineated by the Southwest Corridor, Berkeley Street, and Harrison and Massachusetts avenues. A protected historic district, little has changed since it was laid out in the mid-19th century, making the South End a delightful area to explore.

An impressive ethnic diversity characterizes much of the neighborhood, with scores of nationalities residing here. It is inner-city Boston's most recognizably gay area, although these days preppy young heterosexual families are more common on its streets.

CARLETON COURT PARK

Start this route at the Dartmouth Street exit of **Back Bay/South End Station**, beside Copley Place Mall. Taking up much of Carleton Street is **Carleton Court Park ❶**, which is part of the Southwest Corridor, a 52-acre (21ha) landscaped ribbon of park that runs for several miles southwest toward the suburb of Jamaica Plain.

BRADDOCK PARK

Walk through the park and exit left onto **Braddock Park ❷**. This small street is typical of the leafy residential squares that pepper the South End, all of which have a long, narrow garden, enclosed by wrought-iron railings. The terrace houses that line the sides of the street are entered by steep stoops which often rise a full story to the second floor.

At the end of Braddock Park, you could turn left on Columbus Avenue to enjoy a fine breakfast at **Charlie's Sandwich Shoppe**, see ⑪①.

Below: Charlie's Sandwich Shoppe.

Food and Drink 🍴

① CHARLIE'S SANDWICH SHOPPE
429 Columbus Avenue; tel: 617-536-7669; Mon–Fri 6am–2.30pm, Sat 7.30am–1pm; $
The 'best breakfast in America' is promised at this touchstone of the South End, and they are not kidding. Enjoy their delicious turkey hash and poached eggs and the priceless atmosphere of a traditional diner, with hospitable staff and regular patrons to match.

Above from far left:
South End bar;
neighborhood skyline;
musician in the
Jorge Hernández
Cultural Center.

HARRIET TUBMAN PARK

Cross Columbus Avenue to reach its sharp-angled intersection with Warren Avenue. Here you will find tiny **Harriet Tubman Park ❸**, standing in the lee of the Concord Baptist Church, and graced with two impressive statues. The park is dedicated to the 'Moses of the South,' a runaway slave who organized the 'Underground Railroad,' a network of abolitionists who helped thousands of slaves escape to freedom *(see feature, p.53)*. The red-brick church was built in the 1870s, when many Baptist congregations moved to the South End.

JORGE HERNÁNDEZ CULTURAL CENTER

From the park follow tranquil Pembroke Street south to Tremont Street. Turn right and cross the road to find West Newton Street. At no. 85 is the **Jorge Hernández Cultural Center ❹** (tel: 617-927-0061; www.iba-etc.org; free), housed in a converted 19th-century church. The center provides many services for the South End's large Hispanic community, while the neighboring **Center for Latino Arts** (www.iba-etc. org/claboston) often hosts exhibitions by local and international Latino artists.

Return to Tremont Street and continue west toward the major junction

Naming Boston
Running parallel to the Carleton Court Park is St Botolph Street, named after the monk for whom England's Boston – and also this city – was named.

Above from left: contemporary theater at the Boston Center for the Arts; cupcakes at Flour Bakery.

SoWa Events
The first Friday of every month, between 5 and 9pm, members of the SoWa Artist Guild open up their studios to the public. Twice a year, usually in May and September, they also organize the SoWa Art Walk for a weekend. And on Sundays from mid-May to mid-October a farmers' and crafts market is held in the car park next to 530 Harrison Avenue. See www.sowaartists guild.com for details.

with Massachusetts Avenue. Across the intersection you won't miss the octagonal tower of the old **Chickering Piano Factory**, built in 1850. It was converted into artists' studios and apartments in 1974.

CHESTER SQUARE

Turn left from Tremont Street onto Massachusetts Avenue and walk southwest into **Chester Square** ❺, planned in 1850 as an oval park and once the grandest of the South End's squares. Try to imagine how the square looked then, with a fountain at the center rather than the six lanes of traffic that bisect it now.

Ducking left into the far more pleasant Shawmut Avenue, continue until you reach narrow **Haven Street** ❻, where you should hang a right to discover, at **no. 9**, a charming wooden house (*c.*1830) that is one of only two such remaining in the South End.

Facing the house are the Rutland Washington Community Gardens, small allotments of which there are several in the area. You can pause for refreshments at **Flour Bakery and Café**, see ⑪②, on the corner of Rutland and Washington streets.

BLACKSTONE AND FRANKLIN SQUARES

A block northeast of the Flour Bakery, grassy **Blackstone and Franklin squares** ❼ lie either side of Washington Street. Planned by Charles Bulfinch as a whole oval square in 1801, it was eventually constructed in 1847 as two separate, identical spaces. The cast-iron centerpiece fountains are original. The elaborate edifice that graces Franklin Square at 11 East Newton Street was formerly the St James, one of the city's most elegant hotels. It now serves as apartments.

CATHEDRAL OF THE HOLY CROSS

Further northeast along Washington Street, at no. 1400, it is impossible to miss the towering granite facade of the **Cathedral of the Holy Cross** ❽ (tel: 617-542-5682; www.rcab.org/tourof cathedral; free). Finished in 1875, and still one of the world's largest Gothic cathedrals, it is the seat of the Catholic archbishop in Boston. Pop inside to view the enormous interior, with seating room for 3,500, and many stained-glass windows.

South End History

The marshlands of the South End started to be filled in for construction in the 1830s. By the 1870s the area was fully developed into a grid of red-brick stooped row houses, often laid out, English-style, around squares and small parks.

For a brief period the South End was the place to live, but by the end of 19th century its wealthier residents had decamped to the more fashionable Back Bay, leaving the area largely to the working class and poor immigrants. Many private homes were turned into rooming houses. The area's downward spiral continued well into the 20th century; only in the early 1970s did the South End begin to appeal to 'urban pioneers', who saw the intrinsic value of the run-down buildings and were willing to restore them.

SOWA

Turn right beside the cathedral into Union Park Street, continuing to the junction with Harrison Avenue where you should turn left. You are now in the heart of hip **SoWa** (South of Washington), where warehouses have been converted to galleries, artist studios, loft-style apartments, restaurants, and shops.

SoWa's focal point is **no. 450 Harrison Avenue ❾**, which hosts 50-plus artists' studios and exhibition spaces. There are several other galleries around here too, including one in the art-lover's bookstore **Art Libris** (500 Harrison Avenue), which specializes in out-of-print art books.

PETERS PARKS

From Harrison Avenue follow little Perry Street northwest back to Washington Street. Dead ahead is recently relandscaped **Peters Park ❿**, with its striking Soul Revival mural.

Turn left and then, after the park, right into Waltham Street. At **no. 46** is another collection of artists studios and galleries that you may want to check out.

UNION PARK

Where Waltham Street meets Shawmut Avenue turn left. At the next corner is the **South End Buttery**, see ⑪③. Immediately opposite is delightful **Union Park ⑪**, created in 1851, and the best-preserved of the South End's historic squares.

BOSTON CENTER FOR THE ARTS

A few steps from Union Park's northern end is Tremont Street and the South End's highest density of restaurants. Turn right and cross the street to arrive at the **Boston Center for the Arts ⑫** (539 Tremont Street; tel: 617-426-5000; www.bcaonline.org), housing artists' studios, galleries, and four theaters.

Part of the complex is the unusual **Cyclorama**. Built in 1884 to house a gigantic circular painting (400 x 50ft/ 122 x 15m) of the Battle of Gettysburg by Paul Philippoteaux, the Cyclorama caused a sensation when it opened. The painting is now shown in Gettysburg, but the space is still used for events, and you can usually pop inside for a look.

From here head north up Clarendon Street and cross back over Columbus Avenue to find another entrance to Back Bay/South End Station.

Why Washington is Wide

If you are wondering why Washington Street is so wide, it is because it once had an elevated train line – the Washington Street 'El,' – running along it. Built at the turn of the 19th century, and one of the first of its kind in the US, the line was demolished in the 1980s to be replaced by the Orange Line of the submerged T.

Food and Drink

② FLOUR BAKERY AND CAFÉ
1597 Washington Street, South End; tel: 617-267-4300; www.flourbakery.com; Mon–Fri 7am–9pm, Sat 8am–6pm, Sun 9am–3pm; $
The line at lunchtime nearly goes out the door for this popular café's lattes and gourmet sandwiches like lamb and curried tuna. Also at 12 Farnsworth Street (tel: 617-338-4333; Mon–Fri 7am–7pm, Sat 8am–6pm), around the corner from the Children's Museum on walk 10 *(see p.75)*.

③ SOUTH END BUTTERY
312 Shawmut Avenue; tel 617-482-1015; www.southendbuttery.com; daily 6.30am–6.30pm; $
Service can be sluggish, but that does not stop the crowds flocking to this corner café that specializes in great coffee, loose-leaf teas, and fresh baked goods. Pavement tables provide a ringside seat onto Union Square.

WATERFRONT AND FORT POINT

Now that the elevated expressway has been buried, Boston is rediscovering its Waterfront. Stroll along part of the HarborWalk on this route from Faneuil Hall-Quincy Market, past the fantastic New England Aquarium, to the new Institute of Contemporary Art in the upcoming Fort Point district.

Above: Columbus gives his name to a Waterfront park.

Revolutionary Spark

Three ships laden with tea were moored at Griffins Wharf on December 16, 1773, when patriots disguised as Mohawk Indians boarded them and threw all 340 chests of their cargo into the harbor. This was the most flamboyant act of defiance against the British Parliament for its manipulation of taxes, such as that on tea, to favor British interests. It was 'the spark that ignited the American Revolution.'

DISTANCE 3 miles (5km)

TIME A half day

START Government Centre T Station

END World Trade Centre T Station

POINTS TO NOTE

Allow for a full day if you plan to visit the Aquarium, the Children's Museum, and the ICA. The Children's Museum in particular will likely represent a fair outlay of time and energy for youngsters, so is best set aside as a separate destination, or at least one that follows lunch or a rest period. The weekend is a busy time to visit these places, so go on a weekday if possible. Entry to the Children's Museum is only $1 Friday 5–9pm, and the ICA is free Thursday from 5–9pm.

Until the second half of the 19th century Boston was the busiest port in the nation. Warehouses and counting houses occupied a dozen wharves at which clippers unloaded and loaded their cargoes. In 1878 the construction of Atlantic Avenue severed the finger-like piers from the rest of the city, a process completed with the building in the 1950s of the raised Fitzgerald Expressway. Boston turned its back on its patrimony, and the Waterfront went into seemingly terminal decline.

A reprieve came in the 1970s with the restoration of Faneuil Hall and Quincy Market. Abandoned warehouses were transformed into condominiums. Berths once occupied by barques and brigantines became home to elegant cabin cruisers and sleek sloops. Offices, hotels, restaurants, and museums were also built, and the longshoremen, truckers, and Irish laborers of old were replaced with realtors, lawyers, and tourists.

Now that the Big Dig has buried the Expressway *(see p.13)*, the Waterfront is again joined to the city and being rediscovered thanks to development around the Fort Point Channel and the HarborWalk project *(see feature, p.75)*.

FANEUIL HALL-QUINCY MARKET

Emerge from **Government Center T Station** to the plaza in front of City Hall *(see p.30)*, descend a flight of steps, cross Congress Street, and dive into the retail heaven of the **Faneuil Hall-Quincy Market ❶** complex. Faneuil

Hall is covered in walk 1 *(see p.30)*. Adjoining Quincy Market is named after mayor Josiah Quincy, who came up with the idea for the 1826-vintage marketplace. Much like London's Convent Garden, meat and produce were sold here for 150 years before the buildings were renovated to host the scores of souvenir stalls and boutiques found today. A tourist magnet, with frequent performances by buskers, Quincy Market consists of three long buildings. Eateries abound, including historic **Durgin Park**, see ⑪①, in North Market.

COLUMBUS PARK

Leave the Faneuil Hall-Quincy Market carnival behind and head toward the water, crossing the strip of park that has replaced the buried expressway to arrive at **Columbus Park ②**. A trellised walkway leads to the Waterfront, which at this point has been landscaped into a romantic area of cobblestones, bollards, and anchor chains. On the left stretches **Commercial Wharf** with its granite warehouse. This massive structure, in which the second set of sails for the USS *Constitution (see p.38)* was made, is now a condominium complex.

Above from far left: lobster weather vane; rotunda at Quincy Market; Columbus Park.

Food and Drink 🍴
① DURGIN PARK
340 North Market, Faneuil Hall; tel: 617-227-2038; Mon–Sat 11.30am–10pm, Sun 11.30am–9pm; $$
Little has changed at Durgin Park since it opened in 1827. Still the same pressed-tin ceilings and mosaic-tile floor, still the same Yankee-style cooking (think shepherd's pie and homemade fish cakes) served at communal tables in huge portions.

Below: for Yankee-style cooking.

LONG WHARF

Immediately to the south of Columbus Park is **Long Wharf ❸**. When built in 1710 the wharf extended from near the Old State House *(see p.29)* past the towering Custom House (now a hotel) to the harbor. Gaze out from the esplanade at the end of the wharf to East Boston and the planes taking off from Logan Airport. These are the successors to the swift clippers that once sailed around the globe from this spot. Setting sail from Long Wharf is still possible, either on ferries to Provincetown *(see p.92)*, the Charlestown Navy Yard *(see p.37)*, or the Harbor Islands *(see p.76)*.

Below: cruise ship.

(see p.29) ... *(see p.92)* ... *(see p.37)* ... *(see p.76)*

Food and Drink 🍴

② CHANNEL CAFÉ

300 Summer Street; tel: 617-426-0695; www.channel-cafe. com; daily 8am–3pm, Fri also 5–10pm; $$

An off-the-beaten-track Fort Point gem, Channel Café features mismatched furniture, vegetarian-friendly food, and an adjoining art gallery. The mushroom ravioli and freshly baked cookies are legendary.

③ THE BARKING CRAB

Fort Point Landing, 88 Sleeper Street; tel: 617-426-2722; www.barkingcrab.com; Sun–Wed 11.30am–11pm, Thur–Sat 11.30am–1am; $$

A red-and-yellow tent covers shared bench tables at this casual shack-like place serving mainly seafood. It can get very crowded on summer evenings; if it is busy try the nearby branch of The Daily Catch *(see p.33)*.

④ LTK BAR AND KITCHEN

225 Northern Avenue; tel: 617-330-7430; www.ltkbarand kitchen.com; daily 11am–1am; $$

LTK, or 'Legal Test Kitchen,' is the experimental outpost of Boston's popular seafood chain, Legal Sea Foods. Its high-tech design (including iPod docks at the table) is apt for the up-and-coming South Boston Seaport area, and the menu has multicultural options such as sushi and Vietnamese *pho*.

NEW ENGLAND AQUARIUM

Beside Long Wharf is Central Wharf, on which stands the excellent **New England Aquarium ❹** (tel: 617-973-5200; www.neaq.org; Mon–Fri 9am–5pm, Sat–Sun 9am–6pm; charge). Inside, the Giant Ocean Tank rises three stories high. A ramp encircling the tank takes visitors past more than 70 wall tanks containing a plethora of weird and wonderful fish, as well as turtles and sharks. You can see three species of penguin and two varieties of seal as well. The Aquarium also runs its own whale-watching cruises *(see feature, p.77)*.

Located just across the plaza from the Aquarium is the six-story-high **3D IMAX Theater** (daily 10am–10pm; charge), which shows spectacular films of the natural world's wonders.

BOSTON TEA PARTY SHIPS AND MUSEUM

From Central Wharf continue south past India and Rowes wharves, the latter home to the swish Boston Harbor Hotel *(see p.113)*. Some harbor cruises also depart from here.

Fort Point Channel now intersects the Waterfront. This area was the bustling transfer point for many New England industries during the latter years of the 19th century.

Staying on the Downtown side of the channel, continue past the pedestrian Northern Avenue Bridge and Evelyn Moakley Bridge to the Congress Street Bridge. On a short wharf in the middle of the bridge are the **Boston Tea Party Ships and Museum** ❺ (http://boston teapartyship.com). The museum has been closed for several years after a fire; it is scheduled to reopen in summer 2009, when it will include full-size replicas of the tall ships *Dartmouth* and *Eleanor*, and the restored brig *Beaver*.

CHILDREN'S MUSEUM

On the eastern side of Congress Street Bridge the iconic giant **Hood Milk Bottle** *(see p.14)* stands outside the fantastic **Boston Children's Museum** ❻ (300 Congress Street; tel: 617-426-8855; www.bostonchildrensmuseum. org; daily 10am–5pm, Fri until 9pm; charge). Hands-on installations, including a three-story climbing sculpture and many games, will thrill kids of all ages. Also here is a complete two-story Japanese silk merchant's home, a gift from Kyoto, Boston's sister city.

If you need some refreshment after all the hands-on fun, try **Channel Café**, see ⑪②, a block south on Summer Street, or **The Barking Crab**, see ⑪③, north between the Evelyn Moakley and Northern Avenue bridges.

INSTITUTE OF CONTEMPORARY ART

From The Barking Crab continue north right around the water's edge and past the Joseph Moakley Federal Courthouse. This area is the South Boston Seaport; over the next few years the empty lots here are going to be developed into the city's fanciest waterside residential district. Already constructed is the dramatic glass-sheathed structure that is the new home of the **Institute of Contemporary Art** ❼ (100 Northern Avenue; tel: 617-927-6613; www.ica boston.org; Tue–Sun 10am–5pm, Thur–Fri until 9pm; charge). There are some really innovative and challenging exhibitions here, but the star of the show is the view back to the Downtown skyline from the museum's forecourt.

For another taste of the Seaport district's flashy new future, continue to the eastern end of Northern Avenue to find **LTK Bar and Kitchen**, see ⑪④. Silver Line buses from the nearby World Trade Centre T Station will take you back to the city center.

Above from far left: Rowes Wharf; at the New England Aquarium; Custom House; exhibit at the Institute of Contemporary Art.

Below: Boston Children's Museum.

HarborWalk

The HarborWalk (www.bostonharborwalk.com) stretches 47 miles (76km) from Chelsea Creek, north of Boston, through Charlestown, North End, Downtown, and South Boston to south of Dorchester. Designed to provide access to the restored Boston Harbor, the route hugs the coastline using established walkways as well as new paths. Nearly 38 miles (61km) of the route, also suitable to cycle, have been completed. You can download audio tours from the website to listen to as you follow the route, marked by a blue line.

HARBOR ISLANDS

A summer trip to one or several of the 17 islands in the Boston Harbor Islands National Recreation Area promises a blissful escape from the city to discover nature and historic monuments that few Bostonians know about.

DISTANCE 7 miles (11km)
TIME A full day
START/END Aquarium
T Station/Long Wharf
POINTS TO NOTE

The above distance is from Boston to Georges Island. Harbor Express (tel: 617-222-6999; www.harborexpress. com) runs ferries to the islands from Long Wharf ($14) from early May to mid-October. It takes 30 minutes to reach Georges Island from where Gallops, Lovells, Peddocks, Grape, and Bumpkin islands are between 15 to 30 minutes away using the inter-island shuttle ($5). Alternatively, go straight to Spectacle Island (15min) from where it is possible to connect to Georges.

Camping

Three islands – Lovells, Grape, and Bumpkin – allow camping from late June to early September for a small fee. Reservations should be made with the Department of Conservation and Recreation (tel: 617-727-5290, toll free: 1-877-422-6762; www.mass.gov/dcr/parks/metroboston/harbor.htm).

Boston Harbor is dotted with 34 islands, 17 of which are protected within a state park. They are all wonderful places to relax and enjoy crowd-free hiking, fishing, swimming, and kayaking, as well as a host of other activities. Check the calendar on the website of Boston Harbor Islands (tel: 617-223-8666; www.bostonislands. org) for scheduled events, ranging from shows by the Boston's Children's Theater, jazz performances, and guided ranger walks, including one on Grape Island, every Sunday, where the rangers lead visitors wild-berry-picking.

This daytrip route, possible from mid-June to September 1 when the inter-island ferry operates, takes you to three of the islands: Georges, Lovell, and Spectacle. Four others – Bumpkin, Grape, Hull, and Peddocks – are also accessible on the inter-island ferry, while others, such as Little Brewster, can be reached by ferries direct from the city.

GEORGES ISLAND

From the Aquarium T Station walk the short distance west to **Long Wharf ❶**, where you can board the 9am ferry to Georges Island. The gateway to the other Harbor Islands, **Georges Island ❷** is also the site of Fort Warren, built in 1833; take one of the ranger-led tours around the abandoned complex that once was a training ground for Union soldiers and a prison for Confederate captives. There is a large picnic area here (with restrooms and a snack bar), as well as magnificent views of the Boston skyline and surrounding islands.

LOVELLS ISLAND

Board the 12.50pm inter-island ferry from Georges to **Lovells Island ❸**. Here you can explore the ruins of Fort Standish, search out diverse wildlife, relax on inviting beaches, and wander rocky shores upon which several ships were wrecked. Lovells is one of three islands on which camping is permitted.

SPECTACLE ISLAND

Take the 3.50pm inter-island ferry back to Georges, switching immediately to the ferry for **Spectacle Island ❹**. This is the closest of the park's islands to the city and features a marina, visitor center, café, and life-guarded swimming beach. Follow part of the island's 5 miles (8km) of walking trails that lead to the top of a 157ft (48m) hill offering panoramic views. There are direct ferries from Spectacle Island to Long Wharf and vice versa.

OTHER ISLANDS

Around a mile south of Georges lies **Peddocks Island ❺**, the third-largest harbor island, which has many walking trails, and the remains of Fort Andrews built under the shadow of the Spanish-

American War, and garrisoned during World Wars I and II.

Grape Island ❻ has a campsite, and offers trails along which you are sure to see wildlife and birds among the wild berry trees. Camping is also allowed on **Bumpkin Island ❼**, which lies close to the Hull Peninsula, and hosts the remains of a children's hospital and a farmhouse overgrown with vegetation such as bayberries and wild raspberries.

Only open for tours (reserve via www.zerve.com/harborisland/light) **Little Brewster ❽** is home to Boston Light, the first and oldest lighthouse in the US. The present building was constructed in 1782 after the British had blown up the original (built in 1716) on departing Boston in 1776. It is the only lighthouse in the nation still manned (except in winter) by resident keepers.

Above from far left:
Graves Light; diving whale; Little Brewster and Boston Light.

Food and Drink
Bring a picnic, as the only two islands with any food or drink on them are Georges and Spectacle, both of which host snack bars during the summer season.

Whale Watching

The humpback gathering at the fertile feeding ground Stellwagen Bank, 25 miles (40km) off the Boston coast, is one of the greatest in the world. Minkie whales can be seen too. Boston Harbor Cruises (tel: 617-227-4320; www.bostonharborcruises) and New England Aquarium Whale Watch (tel: 617-973-5277; www.neaq.org/visit/wwatch) run whale-watching tours from Long and Central wharves respectively.

The season starts in April and ends in October, with the peak around June. Cruises take around three hours, and commentary is provided by naturalists. The waters can be rough, so it is a good idea to carry anti-seasickness tablets. Rainwear is useful in April and May, and you should dress warmly even in summer. Whale-watching tours also depart from Gloucester (see p.83), Plymouth (see p.90), and Provincetown (see p.93).

SALEM

*There is more to Salem, 16 miles (26km) north of Boston, than witches, as
you will discover on this walk around one of New England's most historic
towns, which is home to the exceptional Peabody Essex Museum, a treasure
trove of art and culture from around the world.*

Tourist Information

Just off Essex Mall on
New Liberty Street is
the National Park
Visitor Center (tel:
978-740-1650;
www.nps.gov; daily
9am–5pm), where
you can pick up
maps and leaflets,
consult the park
rangers, and
watch an excellent
25-minute film about
the county's history.
Tourist information is
also available at
www.salem.org.

DISTANCE 3½ miles (5.5km)
TIME A full day
START/END Salem Station
POINTS TO NOTE

The distance above is that of the
walking route around Salem. To get
to Salem (16 miles/26km north of
Boston), take a train from the city's
North Station (22 minutes; $5.50)
on the Newburyport/Rockport
Commuter Rail Line (www.mbta.
com). Alternatively, from May to early
November ferries run from Central
Wharf next to the New England
Aquarium in Boston to Blaney Street
Wharf in Salem (tel: 978-741-0220;
www.salemferry.com; one way/
round-trip $12/22). The voyage by
ferry takes 45 minutes.

Salem – the name derives from the
Hebrew *shalom* (peace) – was once one
of the nation's great seaports. It produced the country's first millionaires,
and has the architectural and cultural
heritage to prove it in its McIntire
Historic District and the protected
properties of the Peabody Essex
Museum. However, it does not take
long to find reminders of the activities
most often associated with the town –
the trials and executions of 'witches.'

WITCH DUNGEON MUSEUM

Starting from **Salem Station**, ascend
the steps at the end of the platform,
cross the busy road, and walk down
Washington Street, turning right onto
Lynde Street after two blocks. At no. 16

Food and Drink

① **RED'S SANDWICH SHOP**
15 Central Street; tel: 978-745-3257;
www.redssandwichshop.com;
Mon–Sat 5am–3pm, Sun 6am–
1pm; $
A Salem breakfast institution housed
in the old London Coffee House,
dating from 1698. Arrive early if you
don't want to stand in line. You can
also get grilled sandwiches – great
for a lunchtime snack.

is the **Witch Dungeon Museum** ❶ (tel: 978-741-3570; www.witchdungeon.com; daily 10am–5pm; charge), where you can watch a vividly staged re-enactment of a trial, adapted from a 1692 manuscript, before being guided through the tiny dank dungeons in which the accused were held.

Witch House

The nearby spooky wooden house on the corner of Essex and North streets is the **Witch House** ❷ (tel: 978-744-8815; mid-May–Nov daily 10am–5pm; charge), where trial magistrate Jonathan Corwin cross-examined more than 200 suspected witches; the decor is authentic to the period.

MCINTIRE HISTORIC DISTRICT

Named after Samuel McIntire (1757–1811), one of the foremost American architects of his day, this historic area of Salem, roughly bounded by Federal, Flint, Broad, and Summer/North streets, showcases four centuries of architectural styles.

Historic Houses

Backtrack from the Witch House to Federal Street, where at no. 80 stands the McIntire-designed **Peirce-Nichols House** ❸ (*c.*1782). The house's east parlor has been newly restored and is open for tours by arrangement with the Peabody Essex Museum.

Return to Essex Street and proceed to no. 318, the Georgian-period **Ropes Mansion** ❹, which stands in

a beautiful garden, and features a rare collection of Nanking porcelain and Irish glass. Across the road at no. 337 is the **Salem Athenaeum** (www.salemathenaeum.net; Tue–Wed and Fri 1–5pm, Thur 5–9pm, Sat 10am–2pm; free), a library formed from two previous libraries in 1810.

Turn into quaint Botts Court and walk to Chestnut Street, one of Salem's finest thoroughfares. At no. 34 is the fine **Phillips House** ❺ (tel: 978-744-0440; www.historicnewengland.org; June–Oct Tue–Sun 10am–4pm; charge) where the carriage house contains several antique cars. Retrace your steps back along Chestnut Street to no. 9, the red-brick Federalist gem **Hamilton Hall** ❻ (tel: 978-744-0805; www.hamiltonhall.org; Mon–Fri 9am–3pm; free).

PEABODY ESSEX MUSEUM

From the corner of Chestnut Street turn left onto Summer Street and then right at Essex Street to reach the pedestrian Essex Mall, recognizable by the red paving that matches the red bricks of the buildings. Turn right onto Central Street for **Red's Sandwich Shop**, see ❶❶.

Back on the Mall, reserve a decent block of time to visit the outstanding **Peabody Essex Museum** ❼ (tel: 978-745-9500; http://pem.org; daily 10am–5pm; charge), where an impressive contemporary building by Moshe Safdie displays a fraction of the collection of nearly a million objects.

The museum's origins date back to 1799 and to the art and antiques

Above from far left: the Peabody Essex Museum displays all kinds of maritime artifacts; statue of Roger Conant, founder of Salem (in 1626); Town Hall; bust of John Paul Jones, 'Father of the American Navy,' in the Peabody Essex.

Below: figureheads in the Peabody Essex.

Place to Stay
Salem is so close to Boston that it makes an easy daytrip, but there is so much to see here that you may be tempted to stay overnight. If so, the historic Hawthorne Hotel (18 Washington Street; tel: 978-744-4080; www.hawthornehotel.com) packs plenty of atmosphere and is centrally located just off the Common.

Historic Houses

It is possible to look inside several of the houses in the McIntire Historic District and elsewhere around town by arrangement with the Peabody Essex Museum *(see p.79)*, which manages 22 buildings around Salem, including those in the Phillips Library Neighborhood opposite the museum's main building.

amassed by Salem's seafaring merchants on their global travels. Ships' models, figureheads, nautical instruments, charts, and maps abound, but the museum also has fine antiques from China, Japan, and India, as well as plenty of artifacts from the South Pacific (especially the Solomon Islands) and further afield. There is also a 200-year-old Chinese merchant's home transported from China and rebuilt as part of the museum; entry to this is by timed ticket, and advance reservations are advised.

PHILLIPS LIBRARY

Diagonally opposite the Peabody Essex Museum, a mini architectural park surrounds the red-brick **Phillips Library** ❽ (tel: 978-745-9500; http://pem.org; Wed 10am–5pm, Thur 1–5pm; free), which has a lovely reading room. Notice the stark contrast between the massive columns of the **Andrew-Safford House** (1819; 13 Washington Square) and, behind it, the tiny features

of the **Derby-Beebe Summerhouse** (1799). Also here are the **Gardner-Pingree House** (1804; 128 Essex Street) and, from 1727, the neighboring **Crowninshield-Bentley House**.

WITCH TRIALS MEMORIAL

Follow the short footpath around the eastern side of the Peabody until you reach Charter Street. Here, next to the Burying Point Cemetery – resting place of witch judge John Hathorne – is the most poignant of all Salem's witch-connected sites. The **Witch Trials Memorial** ❾, dedicated by Holocaust survivor and renowned writer Elie Wiesel in 1992, is a contemplative space surrounded by 20 stone benches etched with the trial victims' names, and shaded by a clump of black locust trees – reputedly the kind from which the convicted were hanged.

SALEM MARITIME NATIONAL HISTORIC SITE

From the cemetery, cross Derby Street and walk along its southern side toward **Pickering Wharf** ❿, a touristy collection of stores and restaurants including several antiques shops. The best place to eat here is **Finz**, see ⑪②.

Next to the wharf, the **Salem Maritime National Historic Site** ⓫ focuses on Salem's port. Stop by the **Orientation Center** (tel: 978-740-1660; www.nps.gov; daily 9am–5pm) to find out about ranger-guided tours (charge) to the nearby Custom House, Derby House, and Narbonne

Salem's Witch Hysteria

In 1692, between June and September, Salem fell under a dark spell of mass hysteria, and executed 14 women and six men for witchcraft. You would be forgiven for thinking that the town is still obsessed with witches, for that sad history, portrayed in the Arthur Miller play *The Crucible*, is recalled at many sites – a few historical, others kitsch. Every October the town ramps up its black-arts connection further to run a month-long celebration called Haunted Happenings (www.hauntedhappenings.org), culminating in the crowning of the king and queen of Halloween on the 31st.

House, as well as the *Friendship*, a full-scale replica of a 1797 three-masted East India merchant ship. It is docked at Derby Wharf, one of the few wharves that remain from the 40 of Salem's heyday.

CUSTOM HOUSE

Facing the wharf is the **Custom House** ⑫ (1819), surmounted by a gilded eagle clutching in its claws arrows and a shield, which was made infamous by Nathaniel Hawthorne. Salem's most famous son worked here for three years of 'slavery,' on which he based the introduction to *The Scarlet Letter* (1850).

Adjacent to the Custom House is the **Hawkes House** (1780; not open to the public) and, beyond that, the ochre-brick **Derby House** (1761). The former was built by shipowner Elias Hasket Derby (probably America's first millionaire), to replace the latter, but it was never completed, and was used as a storehouse for booty taken by his Revolutionary privateers.

THE HOUSE OF THE SEVEN GABLES

Continue down Derby Street from the Custom House to reach, at no. 115, **The House of the Seven Gables** ⑬ (tel: 978-744-0991; www.7gables.org; daily July–Oct 10am–7pm, Feb–June and Nov–Dec 10am–5pm; charge), which inspired Nathaniel Hawthorne to write the novel of that name. The small house in which he was born in

1806 has been moved into the grounds. Guides lead you through rooms stuffed with period furniture. Take a breather in the lovely garden afterwards.

From Derby Street you could walk two blocks east to Blaney Street to catch the ferry back to Boston. Otherwise, you can return to Salem Station by cutting through Hardy Street to Essex Street, then walking across **Salem Common** ⑭ to Brown Street, which joins with Church Street, along which you will find the **Lyceum Bar and Grill**, see ⑪③.

Left: Custom House.

Above from far left: Derby House; replica of the *Friendship*; House of the Seven Gables; eagle atop the Custom House.

Food and Drink

② FINZ
76 Wharf Street; tel: 978-744-8485; daily 11.30am–midnight; $$
The best place to enjoy seafood overlooking Salem Harbor. Bypass the tasteless lobster roll in favor of the excellent salmon wrap or great-value haddock sandwich.

③ LYCEUM BAR AND GRILL
43 Church Street; tel: 978-745-7665; www.lyceumsalem.com; Mon–Fri 11.30am–3pm, Sun 11am–3pm, daily 5.30–11pm; $$$
Contemporary American cuisine is served in the elegant surroundings of the building where Alexander Graham Bell made the first long-distance telephone call. Live music Fri and Sat from 9pm.

CAPE ANN

Maritime history, artists' colonies, grand New England mansions, and spectacular coastal scenery are among the attractions of Cape Ann, which is an easy day's drive northeast from Boston.

Place to Stay

The Addison Choate Inn (49 Broadway, Rockport; tel: 1800-245-7543; www.addisonchoateinn.com) is a charming 1850s house that offers modern conveniences such as wi-fi. It has six rooms, and there is a separate cottage with two self-catering units.

Tourist Information

Online tourist information is available at www.seecapeann.com, www.capeannvacations.com, and www.rockportusa.com.

Below: cry of the gull.

> **DISTANCE** 40 miles (63km) from Boston to Rockport
>
> **TIME** A full day
>
> **START** Gloucester
>
> **END** Rockport
>
> **POINTS TO NOTE**
>
> Driving is the best way to get around Cape Ann; the fastest way from Boston is along Route 128, while the most scenic is along MA 127, which follows the coast beyond Salem. Both Gloucester and Rockport are accessible by train from Boston's North Station, and you can get around on Cape Ann Transportation Authority buses (www.canntran.com; tel: 978-283-7916).

3 miles / 5 km

GLOUCESTER

Founded in 1623 by English fishermen, **Gloucester ❶** is the nation's oldest seaport. Unlike Salem, its harbor is still fairly active, with many fishermen now of Portuguese or Italian descent.

If you head into Gloucester along Route 127 from the west, just over the drawbridge spanning the Annisquam Canal you will see the **Fisherman's Monument ❹**, with a helmsman gripping a wheel as he scans the horizon.

Cape Ann Museum

In town begin at **Cape Ann Museum ❺** (27 Pleasant Street; tel: 978-283-0455; www.capeannmuseum.org; Tue–Sat 10am–5pm, Sun 1–4pm; charge), displaying seascapes by the American maritime painter Fitz Hugh Lane and an interesting collection of furniture, silver, and porcelain, in the home of Captain Elias Davis (1804) and the adjoining White-Ellery House (c.1709).

A short walk west along Middle Street, at no. 49, is the **Sargent House Museum ❻** (tel: 978-281-2432; June–Oct Fri–Mon noon–4pm; charge), the home of Judith Sargent and John Murray, which has rooms arranged as they might have looked in 1782 when the house was built. A block south, toward the harbor, you will find several lunch options on Main Street, including **Passports**, see ①.

Further inland, on Main Street, is the attractive Portuguese **Church of Our Lady of Good Voyage ⓓ**, recognizable by its two blue cupolas.

Rocky Neck

From the church, drive around the harbor to East Main Street, passing **Duckworth's Bistrot**, see ①②, and heading on to **Rocky Neck ⓔ** (www.rockyneckartcolony.org), the oldest artists' colony in the US, in a wonderful coastal setting. Rudyard Kipling worked on *Captains Courageous*, about Gloucester fishermen, while staying here.

Eastern Point

On leaving Rocky Neck, turn right onto Eastern Point Road. After about 1 mile (1.6km), take the right fork, even though it is marked 'private.' This is the exclusive enclave of Eastern Point. Open to the public is **Beauport, the Sleeper-McCann House ②** (tel: 978-283-0800; www.historicnewengland.org; June–mid-Oct Tue–Sat 10am–last tour at 4pm; charge), built and furnished between 1907 and 1934 by Henry Davis Sleeper, a collector of American art and antiquities. On the tour you can see rooms Sleeper decorated to cover different periods of American life.

ROCKPORT

About 7 miles (11km) northeast of Gloucester is picturesque **Rockport ③**, once a shipping center for locally cut granite. In the 1920s Rockport was

discovered by artists; it remains an art colony today. Dozen of galleries display works of both local and international artists on Main Street, but what attracts most tourists is **Bearskin Neck ④**. This narrow peninsula, jutting out beyond the harbor, is densely packed with tiny dwellings and old fishing sheds, now converted into galleries, antiques stores, and restaurants.

Enjoy magnificent views of the Atlantic from the breakwater at the end of the Neck, just before which you will pass **My Place by the Sea**, see ①③.

Above from far left:

Gloucester harbor; colorful fishing floats; a photographers' favorite in Rockport is a red lobster shack, visible from Dock Square, called Motif No. 1 because of the infinite number of times it has been photographed and painted.

Whale Watching

Cape Ann Whale Watch (tel: 978-283-5110; www.seethewhales.com) runs whale-watching cruises from Rose Wharf, Gloucester.

Food and Drink 🍴

① PASSPORTS
110 Main Street, Gloucester; tel: 978-281-3680; Mon–Fri 11.30am–9pm, Sat 11.30am–10pm, Sun noon–9.30pm; $
Romantically themed café; great salads, soups, and seafood.

② DUCKWORTH'S BISTROT
197 East Main Street, Gloucester; tel: 978-282-4426; www.duckworthsbistrot.com; Tue–Sun 5–9.30pm; $$
Chef Ken Duckworth's modern American cuisine uses the best of local produce. Many dishes, like grilled organic chicken and sautéed veal cutlets, also come in half-portions. Great for dinner.

③ MY PLACE BY THE SEA
68 Bearskin Neck, Rockport; 978-546-9667; daily May–early Dec 11.30am–3pm, 5–9pm; $$
Fantastic views are guaranteed at this adorable, friendly place serving imaginative modern American cuisine. Good value for lunch, pricier for dinner, when reservations are advised.

LEXINGTON AND CONCORD

Following the 'Battle Road' between Lexington and Concord, west of Boston, will take you past key Revolutionary sites, as well as the beautiful landscape and classic New England locations that inspired American literary giants.

Public Transport

From Boston's Alewife T Station you can take bus no. 62 or 76 to Lexington center. From spring through fall the Liberty Ride tour *(see margin, p.86)* covers the 7 miles (11km) between Lexington and Concord. Alternatively, take a taxi; try Yellow Cabs (tel: 781-862-4600). Trains from Lincoln, a 4-mile (6.5km) walk southwest from Concord, go to Boston's North Station (40 minutes).

DISTANCE 13 miles (20½km) from Boston to Lexington

TIME A full day

START National Heritage Museum, Lexington

END DeCordova Museum and Scupture Park, Lincoln

POINTS TO NOTE

In a car you can visit all the sites in this tour in a day. Consider spending the night in Concord, if you wish to linger at any of the museums or hike the Battle Road Trail. Many sites are shut Sun morning and Nov–mid-April.

LEXINGTON

To reach the start of this tour, head out of Boston on Route 2. Turn right at exit 57 onto Route 4-225. As you approach the center of Lexington there are two sites of historical interest on the left.

National Heritage Museum

A contemporary building houses the **National Heritage Museum ❶** (entrance on Marrett Road; tel: 781-861-6559; www.nationalheritagemuseum.org; Mon–Sat 10am–5pm, Sun noon–5pm; free), featuring changing exhibits of Americana across four centuries.

Food and Drink 🍴

① VIA LAGO

1845 Massachusetts Avenue, Lexington; tel: 781-861-8276; www.vialagocatering.com; Mon–Wed 7am–9pm, Thur–Sat 7am–9.30pm; $
Freshly made sandwiches, light meals, and other snacks are available from this convivial café, which is situated within sight of Battle Green.

② YANGTZE RIVER

25 Depot Square, Lexington; tel: 781-861-6030; www.yangtze lexington.com; Sun–Thur 11.30am–9.15pm, Fri–Sat 11.30am–10.15pm; $
Lexington has a large Chinese population; the fact that many of them frequent this restaurant proves how good the food is. Their dim sum and all-you-can eat buffet brunch at the weekend is a steal at $12.95 per person.

Soon after is the 1635 **Munroe Tavern ❷** (1332 Massachusetts Avenue; tel: 781-862-1703; www.lexington history.org; Sat–Sun mid-April–mid-June, daily mid-June–Oct 11am–3pm; charge), which served as headquarters for the Redcoats and as a hospital on their retreat from Concord.

Battle Green

Drive into the center and park. At one corner of the town common, a tiny triangular park known as **Battle Green ❸**, stands the **Minuteman Statue**, honoring the 77 patriots who faced down the British here, igniting the American Revolution of 1775. They were called Minutemen because they pledged to be ready to fight at a minute's notice.

Opposite on Bedford Street is **Buckman Tavern ❹** (daily 10am–4pm, tours every half-hour; charge), a clapboard building that has been restored to its late 17th-century appearance. After the first battle of the Revolution,

wounded Minutemen were brought here for medical attention. Check out the bullet holes in the door, muskets, original cooking equipment, and 17th-century furniture.

A short walk northwest from Battle Green is **Hancock-Clarke House ❺** (36 Hancock Street; daily May–Oct 10am–4pm; charge). This house, built in 1738, is where, on the night of April 18, 1771, Paul Revere awoke John Hancock and Samuel Adams with the warning that the British were coming.

Before leaving Lexington you could get some refreshments at **Via Lago**, see ⑪①, facing Battle Green, or **Yangtze River**, see ⑪②, around the corner.

BATTLE ROAD

Drive out of Lexington west on Massachusetts Avenue to join Route 2A which shadows **Battle Road ❻**, along which the British, harried by the Minutemen, marched toward Concord.

Above from far left:
Concord in fall; actor in period dress; Minuteman Statue; Battle Road.

Revolution

The battles that started the American Revolution of 1775, leading up to the Declaration of Independence the following year, began in these neighbouring villages, where the Minutemen – a militia of rebels against British rule – faced off against His Majesty's armies, the Redcoats. The first skirmish, at Lexington, did not go well for the Patriots, with eight Minutemen killed. Eleven Redcoats, however, were casualties at Concord.

Tourist Information

Lexington Visitor Center (1875 Massachusetts Avenue; tel: 781-862-1450; www. lexingtonchamber. org; daily Dec–Mar 10am–4pm, Apr–Nov 9am–5pm) is opposite Battle Green next to Buckman Tavern.

Below: The Wayside in Concord.

This whole area is preserved in the Minute Man National Historical Park, through which runs an easy 5-mile (8km) **walking trail** (see dotted line on map). Stop off at the **Minute Man Visitor Center 7** (tel: 978-318-7832; www.nps.gov/mima; Mar–Oct 9am–5pm, Nov until 4pm; free; parking free) to see an excellent multimedia presentation about the start of the Revolution.

CONCORD

The handsome small town of Concord is doubly important. Here is where the second engagement of the Revolution took place, and here, during the first half of the 19th century, lived a handful of renowned literati.

Literary Homes

On the way into Concord is **The Wayside 8** (455 Lexington Road; tel: 978-318-7826; www.nps.gov/mima/wayside; guided tours mid-May–Aug

Wed–Sun, Sept–Oct Fri–Sun, phone ahead for tour times; charge). Louisa May Alcott and her family lived here, as did Nathaniel Hawthorne in later years. Most of the furnishings, though, date from the residence of Margaret Sidney, the author of *Five Little Peppers*.

Down the road is the delightful **Orchard House 9** (tel: 978-369-4118; www.lousiamayalcott.org; Nov–Mar Mon–Fri 11am–3pm, Sat 10am–4.30pm, Apr–Oct Mon–Sat 10am–4.30pm, year-round Sun 1–4.30pm; charge), the Alcott family home from 1858 to 1877, where Louisa wrote *Little Women* and her father, Bronson, founded his school of philosophy.

Concord Museum

Where Lexington Road meets the Cambridge Turnpike (Route 2) is the splendid **Concord Museum 10** (tel: 978-369-9763; www.concordmuseum. org; Mon–Sat 9am–5pm, Sun noon–5pm; charge; free parking). It contains one of the two lanterns that were hung in the Old North Church to warn patriots that the Redcoats were leaving for Concord and Lexington. You can also see Ralph Waldo Emerson's study, which, pretty much in its entirety, was transferred from the wooden Emerson House across the road. The museum also has the largest collection of artifacts associated with the author Henry David Thoreau, including the writing desk from his Walden Pond abode.

Monument Square

Around ¼ mile (400m) further west is **Monument Square 11**, the heart of

Concord. On the square's eastern side is the **Colonial Inn**, see ⑪③.

Park your car, and from the square take a stroll east along Bedford Street (Route 62) to reach **Sleepy Hollow Cemetery** ⑫. In an idyllic setting in the northeastern corner of the cemetery lies Authors' Ridge, the final resting place of Hawthorne, the Alcotts, Emerson, and Thoreau.

Old Manse

Return to Monument Square and drive north for about a mile (nearly 2km) on Monument Street to arrive at the **Old Manse** ⑬ (tel: 978-369-3909; www.oldmanse.org; mid-Apr–Oct Mon–Sat 10am–5pm, Sun noon–5pm; charge), set in immaculate grounds. From this 1770 building the Rev. William Emerson watched the battle for nearby Old North Bridge in 1775. It was later the residence of his grandson, Ralph Waldo Emerson, and then, for three years after their wedding, the Hawthornes.

Old North Bridge

From the Old Manse, stroll to the replica **Old North Bridge** ⑭, spanning the Concord River. On the other side stands the **Minuteman Statue**, rifle in one hand, ploughshare in the other. Emerson's immortal words, 'The shot heard 'round the world,' are inscribed on the plinth. On a hill overlooking the bridge is the **North Bridge Visitor Center** (tel: 978-369-6993; daily 9am–5pm).

Return to the centre of Concord and Main Street to find **Main Streets Market and Café**, see ⑪④.

WALDEN POND

From here, travel south out of town along Walden Street, which crosses Route 2, for 1½ miles (2½ km) to hit **Walden Pond** ⑮ (parking charge), which inspired Thoreau's memoir *Walden* (1854). It takes about an hour to circle the relatively small pond on foot. The best time to visit is in the fall. During summer the pond is a popular swimming spot. A cairn of stones stands alongside the site where the writer lived in a cabin between 1845 and 1847.

GROPIUS HOUSE

Continue south from Walden Pond and, after half a mile, turn left on Baker Bridge Road to reach at no. 68 the **Gropius House** ⑯ (tel: 781-259-8098; www.historicnewengland.org; June–mid-Oct Wed–Sun 11am–4pm, rest of year Sat–Sun only; tours on the hour; charge). This was the first building the German architect designed on arriving in the US in 1937; it expresses Bauhaus principles of function and simplicity.

DECORDOVA MUSEUM AND SCULPTURE PARK

Another mile or so leads to the superb **DeCordova Museum and Sculpture Park** ⑱ (51 Sandy Pond Road, Lincoln; tel: 781-259-8355; www.decordova.org; sculpture park daily 7am–7pm; museum Tue–Sun 11am–5pm; charge), showcasing temporary exhibitions of modern art and sculpture in 35 acres (14ha) of splendid grounds.

Below: Thoreau; replica of the author's cabin.

PLYMOUTH

Head south of Boston to Plymouth to see the spot where 102 pilgrims landed in December 1620, a replica of the ship on which they sailed, and a living recreation of the village in which they lived.

Getting Around
GATRA buses can get you around Plymouth's further-flung sites, but a more convenient option is to take a taxi: try Seabreeze (tel: 508-888-0774), Patriot Cabs (tel: 508-747-1702, or South Shore Taxi (tel: 508-406-8908). From May to September Plymouth Rock Trolley Co. (tel: 508-747-4161; www. plymouthrocktrolley. com) runs narrated trolley tours of the town's major sites on the hour daily between 10am and 4pm, starting at Plymouth Rock.

DISTANCE 40 miles (64km) from Boston to Plymouth; walk: 1½ miles (2.5km)

TIME A full day

START/END Plymouth Waterfront Tourist Information Center

POINTS TO NOTE

If driving, head south out of Boston along Route 1-93, then Route 3, taking exit 6A for Plymouth center. There are direct trains to Plymouth, but the service is very limited and the station is about 2 miles (3km) from the town center. It is better to take one of the more frequent trains to Kingston, from where GATRA buses (tel: 1800-483-2500; www.gatra.org) run to the corner of Memorial Drive and Court Street in Plymouth's center. Alternatively, Plymouth and Brockton buses (tel: 508-746-0373; www.p-b.com) run from Boston to Plymouth's bus depot, just off Route 3 around 2 miles (3km) southwest of Plymouth Rock.

Below: Jenney Grist Mill.

Named after the port town in England from where the Pilgrims had sailed, Plymouth (originally spelled Plimoth) was the first permanent settlement in New England. It initially proved a benighted home for the immigrants, about half of whom died in the first winter though starvation and exposure to the elements. Only with the aid of the Native American tribes did the remaining settlers survive and begin to prosper, leading to the first Thanksgiving festival after the successful harvest of 1621.

AROUND PILGRIM MEMORIAL STATE PARK

Begin at the **Waterfront Tourist Information Center ❶** *(see margin, right)*, then proceed south along Water Street toward **Pilgrim Memorial State Park ❷**. The park's focus is **Plymouth Rock**, an underwhelming boulder that was identified in 1741 by a third-generation elder of the Plymouth Church as the rock upon which the Pilgrim Fathers first stepped, in December 1620, on reaching America. Today this mythical site is protected within a classical portico.

Mayflower II
A mere stone's throw from the monument is the *Mayflower II* ❸ (tel: 508-746-1622; www.plimoth.org; Apr–Nov daily 9am–5pm; charge). This boat, a replica of the original *Mayflower*, was built in England, and sailed to Plymouth in 1957. The 104ft (32m) long vessel vividly conveys the hardships that the 102 members of the crew suffered during the original 55-day voyage.

Cole's Hill

Across the road from Plymouth Rock, climb the flight of stone steps up Cole's Hill ❹ where, during their first winter on the continent, the Pilgrims buried their deceased in the dead of night. These were not marked, 'lest the Indians know how many were the graves.' Over the centuries erosion revealed some of these unmarked graves, and the remains were gathered and placed in a sarcophagus that sits atop the hill.

Near the sacrophagus is a fine bronze statue of **Massasoit**, the Wampanoag chief who befriended the Pilgrims, gave them food, and taught them to plant indigenous vegetables.

BESIDE THE TOWN BROOK

Return to Water Street and continue south to nearby **Brewster Gardens** ❺, a pretty park that hugs both sides of the **Town Brook** from which first the Native Americans and, later, the British settlers got their fresh water and herring.

Jenney Grist Mill

Cross the wooden bridge and follow the brook under two road bridges to arrive at **Jenney Grist Mill** ❻ (6 Spring Lane; tel: 508-747-4544; www.jenneygrist mill.org; April–mid-Nov Wed–Mon 9.30am–4.30pm; charge), located on the site of the mill established in 1636 by John Jenney. Corn is still ground here as it was in the Pilgrims' time.

Richard Sparrow House

Turn right off Spring Lane onto Summer Street to find, at no. 42, the oldest home in Plymouth. The **Richard Sparrow House** ❼ (tel: 508-747-1240; www.sparrowhouse.com; Apr–Dec Thur–Tue 10am–5pm), dates from 1640 and is set up so you can see how the early settlers lived. Next door, Sparrow House Pottery offers a colorful range of crafts.

BURIAL HILL

Follow Summer Street to Market Street and turn left into the Town Square, passing the white clapboard building (dating from 1749) that served as the Court House for Plymouth County; it is now a missable museum. Opposite, also recognizable by its white wooden

Above from far left: *Mayflower II*; Union flag atop the ship; Plymouth Rock; clapboard townhouses.

Tourist Information
The Waterfront Tourist Information Center (170 Water Street; tel: 508-747-7533; www. visit-plymouth.com; Apr–Nov 9am–5pm, June–Aug 9am–8pm) is the best place to start your exploration of Plymouth; pick up maps, information about what's on, and even an MP3 player ($5) for a guided walk around the town.

Whale Watching

For a whale-watching trip from Plymouth try Captain John Boats (tel: 1-800-242-2469; www.captjohn.com). The Captain also runs a daily ferry to and from Provincetown (see p.92) between the end of June and the beginning of September.

structure, is the **Church of the Pilgrimage** ❽. Standing between them is the stone-built **First Church of Plymouth** ❾, the longest continually active church in the US.

Burial Hill ❿ (dawn to dusk) rises up behind the First Church. Many of the first settlers, including William Bradford, and John and Priscilla Alden, were buried here. It is also the site of the Pilgrims' first meeting house, watchtower, and fort, whose cannons protected the harbor. There is a good view of the town and harbor from the top of the hill.

MAP ON P.89

LUNCH ON MAIN STREET

Head back downhill to Main Street, Plymouth's central shopping street, where you can turn left to find **Kiskadee Coffee Company**, see ⊕①, and across the road, **Sam Diego's**, see ⊕②.

HISTORIC HOUSES

Take the second right onto North Street. At no. 27 is **Spooner House** ⓫ (tel: 508-746-0012; June–Sept Thur–Fri 2–6pm, Sat 9am–noon; charge), dating from 1749. This is one of three historical houses in town managed by the Plymouth Antiquarian Society, and features 18th-century furnishings and the belongings of the Spooner family, who lived here for two centuries.

Mayflower Society House

Across the road is the impressive white-washed **Mayflower Society House** ⓬ (tel: 508-746-3188; www.themayflowersociety.com; July–Aug daily 10am–4pm, June and Sept–Oct Sat–Sun only; charge), dating back to 1754. Tours of the interior, reflecting the occupants down the centuries, are available by appointment, while behind the house is a library for genealogical research.

From here, retrace your steps back to Main Street which, heading north, becomes Court Street. A lovely place for refreshment is **All Things Tea**, see ⊕③.

PILGRIM HALL MUSEUM

Continue north along Court Street and you will soon arrive at the **Pilgrim**

Food and Drink

① KISKADEE COFFEE COMPANY

18 Main Street; tel: 508-830-1410; www.kiskadeecoffee.com; Mon–Fri 6.30am–6pm, Thur until 8.30pm, Sat–Sun 7.30am–6pm; $

They do coffee here, of course, but also a big range of bagel and panini sandwiches, as well as other tempting freshly baked goods. Free internet is also a plus.

② SAM DIEGO'S

51 Main Street; tel: 508-747-0048; www.samdiegos.com; daily 11.30am–1am; $$

Enjoy tasty Mexican and southwestern cuisine on the terrace of this lively restaurant (housed in a former fire station), and watch the passing parade on Main Street.

③ ALL THINGS TEA

20 Main Street; tel: 508-747-1221; www.allthingstea.net; Wed–Sun noon–5pm; $

A genteel, traditional English-style temple to tea. Enjoy warm scones with a pot from their wide choice of teas and infusions, or opt for the full afternoon tea if you are hungrier.

④ LOBSTER HUT

25 Town Wharf; tel: 508-746-2270; Sun–Thur 11am–8pm, Fri–Sat 11am–9pm; $

Really nothing fancy, but when it comes to enjoying seafood within toe-dipping-distance of the water, then this Plymouth institution is the place to head.

Hall Museum ⑬ (tel: 508-746-1620; www.pilgrimhall.org; Feb–Dec daily 9am–4.30pm; charge) in a handsome Greek Revival building dating from 1824, with a recently opened modern extension. The museum features an extensive collection of memorabilia from the first Pilgrim families, a range of Native American artifacts, and the remains of *Sparrow Hawk*, a sailing ship that was wrecked in 1626.

TOWN WHARF

From the museum, take the next right down Memorial Drive to arrive back at the Tourist Information Center *(see margin, p.89)*. Across the road is the **Town Wharf**, where you could end your Plymouth tour with a seafood meal at the **Lobster Hut**, see ⑪④.

PLIMOTH PLANTATION

If you have time, it is certainly worth making a visit to **Plimoth Plantation** (137 Warren Avenue; tel: 508-746-1622; www.plimoth.org; Apr–Nov daily 9am–5pm; charge), where the year is always 1627 (they use the 17th-century phonetic spelling for Plymouth, as Governor William Bradford did in his diary). From the Town Wharf, follow Water Street southeast then Sandwich Street for about 2km (1¼ miles) to reach the correct turn-off.

In the plantation's English Village actor-guides dressed in authentic 17th-century costumes and speaking in old English dialects assume the roles of specific historical residents of the colony.

Ask Mistress Alden or Captain Standish about such 18th- or 19th-century figures as Paul Revere or George Washington and they will look at you with incomprehension. The guides do not simply stand around waiting for questions, but go about their 1627 work – salting fish, shearing sheep, baking bread in clay ovens, and even playing ninepins. Even the livestock has been painstakingly 'back-bred' to approximate 17th-century barnyard beasts.

Wampanoag Homesite

Another part of the site is the Wampanoag Homesite, which portrays how Native Americans lived in Massachusetts in the 1620s. The Wampanoag – in their language, 'People of the Dawn' – were a seasonally nomadic tribe, hunting inland in fall and winter, and moving to the coast in spring and summer where they fished and grew corn, squash, and beans. It is a rare opportunity to meet native people in traditional dress and find out about their ancient culture and skills.

Above from far left: statue of Massasoit, the Wampanoag chief, on Cole's Hill; Wampanoag dress; pilgrim at Plimoth Plantation; 1627 English Village in the plantation.

Place to Stay
Next to the Mayflower Society House is Whitfield House (26 North Street; tel: 508-747-6735; www.whitfieldhouse.com), dating from 1782. Fireplaces, antique furniture, and three canopy beds in three of its four bedrooms set an appropriate historical tone at this charming B&B.

First Landfall

Despite all the fuss made over Plymouth Rock, history relates that Plymouth was not the Pilgrim Fathers' first landfall in the New World. That honor belongs to Provincetown *(see p.92)*, at the tip of Cape Cod, where a small party landed on November 21, 1620. The group explored Cape Cod by boat, until they discovered Plymouth, which offered a good harbour, high ground on which they could take defensive positions if attacked, fresh water, and fields cleared and abandoned by Native Americans.

PROVINCETOWN

First came the Pilgrim Fathers, later whalers and fishermen, followed by artists, and, most recently, the gay and lesbian community. Now everyone heads to Provincetown, at the hooked tip of Cape Cod, to enjoy its laid-back atmosphere and fantastic national park-protected dunes and beaches.

DISTANCE 115 miles (186km) from Boston to P-town by road; 57 miles (92km) by ferry

TIME A full day

START/END Provincetown's MacMillan Wharf

POINTS TO NOTE

The fastest way to Provincetown is by ferry (*see below right*). If driving, head south out of Boston along Route 1-93, then Route 3, cross the Saga-more Bridge, then follow Route 6, which runs for 60 miles (100km), down the hooked spine of Cape Cod to Provincetown. More scenic is traveling part of the way on Route 6a, running parallel to Route 6 to the west, and passing through several of the Cape's prettiest villages, such as Sandwich and Barnstable. Provincetown is a seasonal destination; many places are closed during much of December and March and all of January and February.

Tourist Information
Maps and other tourist information are available at the Chamber of Commerce (tel: 508-487-3424; www. ptownchamber.com; Jan–Mar Mon and Fri 11am–3pm, Apr–May and Nov–Dec Mon–Sat 10.30am–5pm, June–Oct daily 9am–6.30pm), on the right as you leave Mac-Millan Wharf. See also www.province town.com.

Thick with craft shops, art galleries, stores selling nick-nacks and antiques, cafés, restaurants, and bars, 'P-town' is an unashamed tourist destination, but also, thanks to strict town ordin-ances, a beautiful-looking one. It is no surprise to find that generations of artists have been drawn to P-town and continue to practice here.

An hour-and-a-half ferry ride from Boston (or a two-hour drive), it is possible to make Provincetown a daytrip, although it is far better ex-perienced on an overnight stay. Hiring a bicycle is recommended as distances from one end of P-town to the other are long; try Arnold's (tel: 508-487-0844), just to the left as you leave MacMillan Wharf at 329 Commercial Street, or Ptown Bikes (tel: 508-487-8735; www.ptownbikes.com) at 42 Bradford Street.

FERRY FROM BOSTON

The following tour assumes you will arrive in P-town by ferry. Running between May and October, there are several fast ferries daily (90 minutes; $71 round trip), with little to choose between the services of **Boston Harbor Cruises** (tel: 617-227-4321; www. bostonharborcruises.com), departing from Long Wharf, near the New England Aquarium *(see p.74)*, and **Bay State Cruise Company** (tel: 877-783-3779; www.baystatecruisecompany. com), departing from the World Trade Center on Seaport Boulevard.

MacMillan Wharf

Ferries dock at **MacMillan Wharf**, toward the end of which you will find the **Expedition Whydah** ❶ (tel: 508-487-8899; www.wydah.com; charge), a small museum documenting the remains of the pirate ship *Whydah*, which sank in 1717 off the coast of the Cape. Continue down the wharf, past the many boats offering whale watching and other ocean-going tours, to the Chamber of Commerce office for tourist information *(see margin, left)*. Immediately ahead is Commercial Street, P-town's principal retail thoroughfare.

PILGRIM MONUMENT

Approaching P-town from land or sea, you cannot miss the slender granite tower rising up 252ft 7½in (77m) from High Pole Hill. To reach the **Pilgrim Monument and Provincetown Museum** ❷ (tel: 508-487-1310; www. pilgrim-monument.org; daily Apr–mid-June and mid-Sept–Nov 9am–5pm, mid-June–mid-Sept 9am–7pm; charge), walk inland from Commercial to Bradford Street, then hike up High Poll Hill Road.

Inspired by the Torre del Mangia in Siena and completed in 1910, the monument commemorates the Pilgrims'

stop in Provincetown in 1620 for six weeks before they moved on to Plymouth *(see p.88)*. To get your bearings of P-town's confusing geography, and for a grand 360-degree view of the Lower Cape, it is worth slogging up the tower's 116 steps and 60 ramps. The fascinating museum at the monument's base is strong on local history, and includes a section on the Arctic explorations of townsman Donald MacMillan (1874–1970).

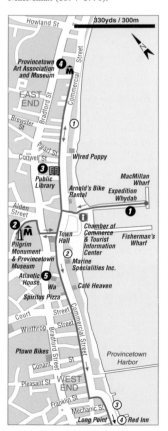

Above from far left: P-town and the Pilgrim Monument behind; typical architecture; browsing the artwork in the Provincetown Art Association and Museum.

Places to Stay
P-town is packed with guesthouses and holiday rentals. Reserve well in advance for the peak July–Aug season. Rates drop substantially out of season. A fine budget option is Provincetown Inn (1 Commerical Street; tel: 508-487-9500; www. provincetowninn. com), a motel-style resort bounded by water on three sides and with its own pool and direct access to the beach. More upmarket, and inland, is The Brass Key (67 Bradford Street; tel: 1800-842-9858; www.brasskey.com), also with a small pool and spa.

Above from left:
tourist cabins; Race Point Lighthouse; *Two Women in White* by Selina Trieff exhibited at the Provincetown Art Association and Museum.

Provincetown Trolley
Usually running between late May and October, the Provincetown Trolley (tel: 508-487-9483) offers a narrated sightseeing tour along Commercial Street and through the Cape Cod National Seashore. You can hop on and off the 40-minute tour along the way. Tours depart from the Town Hall on Commercial Street every half-hour daily between 10am and 4pm.

THE EAST END

Return to Commercial Street and head left toward the **East End**. This is the artistic end of P-town, packed with galleries; you will find a concentration around **The Mews**, see ⑪①. Before reaching there, pop into the **Public Library ❸** (356 Commercial Street; tel: 508-487-7094; www.ptownlib. com; Mon and Fri 10am–5pm, Tue and Thur noon–8pm, Wed 10am–8pm, Sat 10am–2pm, Sun 1–5pm; free), surely the only library in the world to house a full-masted half-size replica of an Indian Schooner (the *Rose Dorothea*).

Provincetown Art Association

At no. 379 you can get a caffeine boost at **Wired Puppy** (tel: 508-487-0017; www.wiredpuppy.com), then power on to the **Provincetown Art Association and Museum ❹** (PAAM; tel: 508-487-1750; www.paam.org; May–Sept Mon–Thur 11am–8pm, Fri 11am–10pm, Sat–Sun 11am–5pm, Oct–May Thur–Sun noon–5pm; charge) at no. 460. Top-class exhibitions are staged here, maintaining a tradition that started in 1899 with the founding of the Cape Cod School of Art by Charles Hawthorne.

THE WEST END

Return to the center of town and continue along Commercial Street toward the **West End**. On the way you will pass many P-town mainstays, including **Ross's Grill**, see ⑪②, at the Whaler's Wharf; the surplus store **Marine Specialties Inc.** at no. 235, an Ali Baba's cave of sale items; the historic **Atlantic House ❺** (4 Masonic Place; tel: 508-487-3821), better known as the A-House, once home to the playwright Eugene O'Neill and now an eternally popular gay bar; the interior-design store **Wa** (tel: 508-487-6844; www.waharmony.com), at no. 220, which has a lovely oriental-style garden to the rear; **Café Heaven** (tel: 508-487-9639) at no. 207, a great place for breakfast or lunch; and, at no. 190, **Spiritus Pizza** (tel: 508-487-2808), where everyone heads at 1am once the town's clubs have shut.

Right: classic Cape Cod detail.

Coastal Cottages

Further down Commercial Street there are a few antiques stores, but once you have followed the road left around the Coast Guard Station the shops are replaced by guesthouses and private residences, with the sole restaurant being **Sal's Place**, see ⑪③. The numerous weatherboard cottages surrounded by flowergardens here are a sight to behold, particularly in the crisp ocean light. Particularly picturesque is the aptly named **Red Inn**, see ⑪④, on whose lawns you will often see art classes being held.

CAPE COD NATIONAL SEASHORE

There are pleasant beaches either side of MacMillan Wharf, but P-town's best strips of sand are part of the **Cape Cod National Seashore (CCNS)**, including **Long Point ❻**, the slender sandbar that hooks back into Cape Cod Bay. You can reach here by walking across the breakwater at the far western end of Commercial Street; the uneven stones can make the crossing a challenge. Once on Long Point you can aim either right to the lighthouse at Wood End or left to the lighthouse on the tip of the sandbar – going in this direction you will pass the P-town nudist beach.

Along the Coast

If you are on a bicycle or in a car, consider exploring more of the beaches and dunes. Heading north along the coast toward the Atlantic side of the Cape, **Herring Cove Beach ❼** is popular with families and a fine spot to watch

sunsets. Further around, and pinpointed by another lighthouse, is **Race Point Beach ❽**, behind which is P-town's airport. You will get a fine view of the area from the observation deck above the **Province Lands Visitor Center** (tel: 508-487-1256; www.nps.gov/caco; daily May–Oct 9am–5pm; free), where can find out about ranger-led walks around the national park. Note if you bring your car or bike into the national park area there is a small charge.

If you came by ferry, head back to Macmillan Wharf to return to Boston.

Long Point Homes
For the first half of the 19th century Long Point was home to a fishing community of 38 houses. As the fishing around here dried up, the homes were put on rafts and floated across to P-town, where many of them still stand, marked by blue-and-white enamel plaques.

Food and Drink

① THE MEWS
429 Commercial Street; tel: 508-487-1500; www.mews.com; daily 6–10pm; $$$
As if the classy menu and ambience – with the lower level offering dining right beside the beach – is not sufficient, The Mews also sports New England's largest selections of vodka.

② ROSS'S GRILL
Whaler's Wharf, 237 Commercial Street; tel: 508-487-8878; www.rossgrilltown.com; Thur–Mon 11.30am–3.30pm, 5.30–10pm; $$$
Intimate and friendly, Ross's is the epitome of relaxed fine dining, with excellent bistro-style dishes such as steak frites and crispy Tuscan cod. Offers a wide selection of wines by the glass.

③ SAL'S PLACE
99 Commercial Street; tel: 508-487-1279; www.salsplaceof provincetown.com; May–Oct daily 5.30–10pm; $$
When other places are booked up it is often possible to squeeze in at Sal's, an authentic Italian joint in the West End with a romantic beachside terrace. The portions are huge.

④ RED INN
15 Commercial Street; tel: 508-487-7334; www.theredinn.com; May–Oct daily 5.30–late, Fri–Sun 11.30am–3pm, Nov–Apr Sat–Sun dinner only; $$$
One of the most pleasant places to dine in P-Town is this elegant West End inn with beautiful gardens and a prime beachside position. The cuisine is modern American, and portions are generous. There is also accommodation here, if you decide to stay over.

DIRECTORY

A user-friendly alphabetical listing of practical information, plus hand-picked hotels and restaurants, clearly organized by area, to suit all budgets and tastes.

A

ADMISSION FEES

Boston Card: tel: 1-800-887-9103; www.gobostoncard.com. Boston Travel and Tourism's one-, two-, three-, five- or seven-day visitor pass offers unlimited admission to over 60 attractions and tours in and around Boston, including several popular sightseeing tours and museums. Cards can be bought online or at the Bostix booths at Faneuil Hall and Copley Square *(see margin, p.19)*, and the Boston Common and Prudential Center visitor information centers *(see p.103)*.

Boston CityPass: tel: 1-888-330-5008; www.citypass.com. This pass covers admission to six top sites, including the Prudential Center Skywalk, Museum of Fine Arts, Museum of Science, and New England Aquarium, as well as discounts at several other attractions and restaurants ($44 adults; $24 youths). It is good for nine consecutive days, and is sold online and at all the above locations.

B

BUSINESS HOURS

Most **offices** are open Monday to Friday 9am to 5pm. Federal and local government offices are usually open weekdays 8.30am to 4.30pm. **Banks** are open weekdays 9am to 4pm. Some are also open on Thursday until 5pm and Saturday 9am to noon.

C

CLIMATE

Boston has four distinct seasons. The first snow generally falls in November and continues intermittently through March. Spring, which can be fleeting, starts in April, and is characterized by crisp, clear days and chilly evenings. June to September can be very hot and humid, although most of the summer is pleasant due to the ocean breeze. Fall is glorious, and the famous New England multicolored foliage peaks in mid-October as the temperature starts to plummet.

Call 617-936-1234 for free daily weather updates, or check online at www.accuweather.com.

CONSULATES

Most embassies are based in Washington, DC, but many countries have consulates in Boston. A complete list can be found at www.state.gov/s/cpr/rls/dpl/32122.htm.

Australia: 55 Thomson Place, 55T3; tel: 617-261-5555; www.dfat.gov.au/missions/countries/usbo.html/.
Canada: 3 Copley Place, Suite 400; tel: 617-262-3760; www.dfait-maeci.gc.ca.
Ireland: 535 Boylston Street; tel: 617-267-9330; www.embassyofireland.org.
Israel: 20 Park Plaza; tel: 617-535-0200; www.israelemb.org/boston.
United Kingdom: 1 Memorial Drive, Suite 1500; tel: 617-245-4500; www.britainusa.com/boston.

Above from far left: lazy afternoon on the bank of the Charles River; motorbike cop.

CRIME AND SAFETY

Boston is one of the safest cities in the US, but visitors should always be vigilant. Areas where crime is a problem, such as Dorchester, Mattapan, and Roxbury, offer few tourist attractions, and are on the fringes of the city. One central area to avoid, especially at night, is south of Washington Street and west of Massachusetts Avenue. Avoid the Fenway Victory Gardens in Back Bay Fens, as violent attacks have been reported here.

CUSTOMS

Anyone over the age of 21 may bring 200 cigarettes, 50 cigars, or 3lbs of tobacco, one liter of alcohol, and a maximum of $100 worth of duty-free gifts. Importing meat products, seeds, plants, or fruits is illegal, as are narcotics. The US permits you to take out anything you wish, but consult with the authorities of your destination country to learn of its customs regulations on entry.

D

DISABLED TRAVELERS

Boston caters well to the disabled traveler, with accessible bathrooms and ramps on public buildings, curbsides, and at most attractions. However, it is also an old city with colonial buildings and cobblestone sidewalks, so despite best efforts it is not always perfect. Check the Massachusetts Bay Transit Authority's website (www.

mbta.com) for public transport access information for disabled travelers, including details of its The Ride service for door-to-door paratransit. For more information call 617-222-3200 or TTY 617-222-5146. Boston's Commission for Persons with Disabilities can be reached on tel: 617-635-3682 or via www.cityofboston.gov/civilrights/disability.asp.

E

ELECTRICITY

The US uses 110–120V, 60-cycle AC voltage (as opposed to the 220–240V, 50-cycle of Europe). Laptops and many travel appliances are dual voltage and will work, but check first. An adapter will be needed for US sockets.

EMERGENCY NUMBERS

Ambulance, Fire, and Police: tel: 911.

G

GAY TRAVELERS

Massachusetts is famous as the first US state to legalize same-sex marriage. In general Boston is a very integrated city, so you will find gays and straights mingling in many city neighborhoods. The South End has the highest concentration of gay bars *(see p.123 for recommendations)*, and is also the home of the annual Boston Pride parade that culminates in a huge carnival. Somerville and Jamaica

Gay media include
Bay Windows (www.
baywindows.com) a
free weekly news-
paper covering
Boston news, gay
culture, and nightlife,
and *New England
Blade* (www.innews
weekly.com), which
has a wider New
England focus.
The website Out in
Boston (www.out
inboston.com) is
also useful.

Plain are popular areas for lesbians to hang out.

The **Greater Boston Business Council** (www.gbbc.org) is the city's gay chamber of commerce, with information on businesses owned, operated, or supported by the local gay community.

H

HEALTH AND MEDICAL CARE

Foreign visitors needing medical attention can face stiff bills for one night in a hospital in a semi-private room. It is advisable to arrange medical insurance before leaving home.

Hospitals

Brigham & Women's Hospital, 75 Francis Street; tel: 617-732-5500; www.brighamandwomens.org.
Mount Auburn Hospital, 330 Mount Auburn Street; tel: 617-492-3500; www.mountauburn.caregroup.org.
Massachusetts General Hospital, 55 Fruit Street; tel: 617-726-2000; www.massgeneral.org; Mon–Fri 8.30am–8.30pm. Non-emergency walk-in clinic.
Tufts Medical Center, 800 Washington Street; tel: 617-636-5000; www.tufts-nemc.org.

Emergency Dental Care

Tufts Dental School, 1 Kneeland Street; tel: 617-636-6828; http://dental.tufts.edu; Mon–Fri 9–10.30am, 1–2.30pm. Emergency walk-in clinic with limited admissions.

Medical Hotlines

Beth Israel Deaconess Hospital, tel: 617-667-7000; www.bidmc.harvard.edu.
Massachusetts Eye and Ear Infirmary, tel: 617-523-7900; www.meei.harvard.edu.
Aids hotline, tel: 1-800-235-2331; Mon–Thur 9am–9pm, Fri 9–7.30pm; www.aac.org.

Pharmacies

Several branches of CVS (www.cvs.com) are open 24 hours, including:
CVS Pharmacy, 55 Charles Street; tel: 617-227-0437.
CVS Pharmacy, 35 White Street, Cambridge; tel: 617-876-5519.

I

INTERNET

Wireless internet access is almost ubiquitous in cafés and many student-type hangouts. Many places charge a fee for increments of an hour to 24 hours, but you can also find free hotspots (www.ilovefreewifi.com) throughout the city.

Boston Public Library, 700 Boylston Street; tel: 617-536-5400; www.bpl.org; Mon–Thur 9am–9pm, Fri–Sat 9am–5pm. Free wireless connections to the Library's internet service in all 28 branches, with direct plug-in ports available in Bates Hall in the Central Library.

Cambridge Public Library, 359 Broadway, Cambridge; tel: 617-349-

4040; Mon–Thur 9am–9pm, Fri–Sat 9am–5pm, Sun 1–5pm. Free wireless access in all the branches, with a few internet computer stations available on a first-come-first-served basis for 20-minute or one-hour sessions. Users are allowed up to 15 pages of free printing per day.

L

LEGAL MATTERS

In the unfortunate event you are arrested, you are legally allowed to remain silent, and are entitled to free legal representation, provided by the state, if you cannot afford it yourself. You are also entitled to a single phone call. If you do not have family, friends, or a lawyer that can be of assistance, call your embassy or consulate. The legal drinking age in Massachusetts is 21, and driving under the influence is a serious offense that will result in stiff fines and jail time.

LOST PROPERTY

Most establishments operate their own lost-and-found department, but if you lose something in a public area, go to the local police station to see if it has been handed in.

Lost or Stolen Credit Cards
AMEX: tel: 1-800-528-2121
Diners Club/Carte Blanche: tel: 1-800-234-6377
MasterCard: tel: 1-800-307-7309
Visa: tel: 1-800-336-8472

M

MAPS

Insight Guides' FlexiMap Boston is laminated for durability and easy folding, and contains travel information as well as exceptionally clear cartography. Rubel BikeMaps (tel: 617-776-6567; www.bikemaps.com) produces great cycling maps for routes in and around Boston.

MEDIA

Newspapers: The city has two daily newspapers: the broadsheet *Boston Globe* (www.boston.com) and the tabloid *Boston Herald* (www.boston herald.com). The 'Sidekick' supplement in Thursday's *Globe* gives events listings for the coming week. The *Christian Science Monitor* (www.cs monitor.com), a prestigious newspaper published in Boston on weekdays, is strong on international news.

Free weekly papers include *The Phoenix* (www.thephoenix.com) and *Weekly Dig* (www.weeklydig.com). Both offer good features, well-written arts and music sections, and full city events listings. There is also the *Improper Bostonian* (www.improper.com), a free weekly lifestyle magazine, and the free bimonthly *Stuff@Night* (www.stuffat night.com). All of these are distributed from sidewalk dispensers.

In shops you can buy *Boston Magazine* (www.bostonmagazine.com), a slick, informative monthly magazine with local features and interviews.

Out of Town News (tel: 617-354-7777) is a kiosk in the middle of Harvard Square that sells a range of national and international publications.

Radio: Stations include WBZ (www.wbz1030.com) on 1030AM for news; WERMD on 850AM for sports; WRKO (www.wrko.com) on 680AM for talk; WCRB (www.wcrb.com) on 102.5FM for classical music; WBCN (www.wbcn.com) on 104.1FM for rock music; and WGBH (www.wgbh.org) public radio on 89.7FM for national programs.

Television: Stations include Channel 2 (www.wgbh.org) for public television; and the national networks CBS on Channel 4 WBZ (www.wbztv.com), ABC on Channel 5 WCVB (www.thebostonchannel.com), NBC on Channel 7 WHDH (www.whdh.com), and Fox on Channel 25 WFXT (www.myfoxboston.com).

MONEY

Major credit and debit cards are widely accepted. Some smaller restaurants accept cash only; they will usually post it in the menu, or you can check with your waiter beforehand. Car rental agencies and some hotels will require you to have a credit card. ATMs are plentiful. Traveler's checks are easily converted to cash at any bank, but you will need your passport to prove your identity. Foreign currency exchange is not handled by all banks; your best bets for this are travel services companies.

Travelex, 745 Boylston Street, Boston; www.travelex.com.
American Express Travel, 1 State Street, Boston; tel: 617-723-8400; 39 J.F. Kennedy Street, Cambridge; tel: 617-868-2600.

P

POST

The main Post Office is at 25 Dorchester Avenue (behind South Station; tel: 617-654-5302; www.usps.gov; daily 24 hours). There are many branches across the city, most open Mon–Fri 9am–5pm, including at Logan Airport. Stamps are available in vending machines in airports, hotels, stores, bus and train stations, as well as online.

PUBLIC HOLIDAYS

All government offices, banks, and post offices close on public holidays. Public transportation does not run as often on these days, but most shops, museums, and other attractions will be open.

Jan 1: New Year's Day
Third Mon Jan: Martin Luther King Day
Third Mon Feb: President's Day
March/April: Easter Sunday
Third Mon Apr: Patriot's Day
Last Mon May: Memorial Day
July 4: Independence Day
First Mon Sept: Labor Day
Second Mon Oct: Columbus Day
Last Thur and Fri Nov: Thanksgiving
Dec 25: Christmas

Smoking
Smoking is banned in all indoor public places across the state, including bars, clubs, and restaurants. In some bars there are outdoor areas set aside for smoking; if not, you have to go out on the street.

T

TELEPHONES

Phone numbers: All telephone numbers have ten digits. The Greater Boston area code, included in the number even when calling within the city, is 617. Surrounding towns use 508 (Plymouth and Provincetown), 781 (Lexington and Concord), and 978 (Salem and Cape Ann). If you are calling outside the local area then a 1 precedes the 10-digit number.

Calling from abroad: To dial Boston from the UK: 00 (international code) + 1 (USA) + a 10-digit number. For calls to other countries from Boston dial the international access code (011), then the country code, city code, and local number. Directory assistance is 555-1212 preceded by 1 and the area code you are calling from or inquiring about; so for Boston call 1-617-555-1212.

Public telephone boxes: The popularity of cell (mobile) phones means you will find few public telephone booths in Boston. Newer cell handsets from Europe and Asia work in US cities, but reception in suburban and rural areas tends to be spotty. This is improving as the US upgrades its cell infrastructure. Pay-as-you-go SIMs that will work in your phone, depending on the model, can purchased from several outlets throughout the city. Main companies are AT&T (www.att.com), Sprint (www.sprint.com), and Verizon (www.verizon.com).

TIME ZONES

Boston is on Eastern Standard Time, which is five hours behind Greenwich Mean Time. The US has four time zones, so Boston is three hours ahead of Los Angeles, two hours ahead of Denver and one hour ahead of Chicago.

TIPPING

Tipping is voluntary, but unlike in Europe service charges are not added to bills. Waiters, taxi drivers, bartenders, etc will expect gratuities, as this supplements their minimum wage pay. Standard is 15 per cent of the bill, with 20 per cent for above-average service and at better restaurants. Doormen, skycabs, and porters receive $1–2 per bag, and chambermaids, $1–2 per night.

TOURIST INFORMATION

The **Greater Boston Convention and Visitors Bureau** (Two Copley Place; tel: 617-536-4100/1-888-733-2678; www.bostonusa.com) runs two visitor centers:
Boston Common Visitor Information Center, 148 Tremont Street; daily 9am–5pm (the booth here marks the start of the Freedom Trail).
Prudential Visitor Center, Center Court, Prudential Center, 800 Boylston Street; Mon–Sat 9am–5pm, Sun 1–5pm.

The **Cambridge Office of Tourism** (4 Brattle Street, Cambridge; tel: 1-800-862-5678/617-441-2884; www.

Above from far left: New Old South Church in silhouette; Fenway Park.

Toilets
Public toilets in Boston are scarce. You can find listings for available facilities and associated cleanliness ratings online (www.boston-online.com/restrooms). The best options are libraries, hotel lobbies, shopping malls or asking politely at a restaurant or café.

cambridge-usa.org; Mon–Sat 9am–5pm) has a booth in the center of Harvard Square (tel: 617-497-1630; Mon–Sat 9am–5pm, Sun 11am–5pm).

Faneuil Hall Marketplace Information Center, south side of Quincy Market; tel: 617-338-2323; www.faneuilhallmarketplace.com/index.html; Mon–Sat 10am–9pm, Sun noon–6pm.

Massachusetts Office of Travel and Tourism, 10 Park Plaza, Suite 4510; tel: 617-973-8500; www.massvacation.com; Mon–Fri 9am–5pm. Supplies information on Boston and the state.

Massport International Information Booth, Logan International Airport (Terminal E); summer noon–8pm; winter noon–6pm.

There are two **National Park Service Visitor Centers** (www.nps.gov/bost), both open daily 9am to 5pm: Charlestown Navy Yard (tel: 617-242-5601); and Downtown (15 State Street, opposite Old State House; tel: 617-242-5642).

TRANSPORTATION

Arrival by Air

Logan Airport (tel: 1-800-235-6426; www.massport.com) has five terminals (A to E). Airlines do not necessarily use the same terminal for domestic and international flights. There are free shuttle buses that are wheelchair-lift-equipped and run between the terminals. In addition, an on-call (tel: 617-561-1770) lift-equipped van serves all Logan Airport's facilities; it can be requested from any Public Information Booth at the arrivals level/baggage claim.

Airport to City

Logan is only 3 miles (4.8km) from Downtown Boston. **Logan Shuttle** buses (www.massport.com) connect the terminals' arrival levels with the MBTA Blue Line (T-stop: Airport; tel: 617-222-3200; www.mbta.com). It takes about 10 minutes to Downtown, where you can transfer to the Green Line (T-stop: Government Center) and Orange Line (T-stop: State Street).

The **Silver Line** is a rapid-transit bus service, also part of the MBTA system, which stops at all the airport terminals and connects with the Red Line and Amtrak train (T-stop: South Station), before continuing to the South End.

Taxis are stationed outside each terminal. Fares to the city or to Cambridge are approximately $25 (excluding tip and surcharges) providing there are no major traffic jams. A surcharge that covers the tolls ($5.25) and airport fees ($2.25) is added to any trips going into the city. Also see the Massport website for details of flat fares to suburban areas.

Water shuttles are a delightful way to approach the city, and convenient if you are staying in Downtown, North End, or the Waterfront. Operators include:

T Harbor Express (tel: 617-222-6999; www.harborexpress.com; $1.70). Runs to Long Wharf.

City Water Taxi (tel: 617-422-0392; www.citywatertaxi.com; Apr–Dec Mon–Sat 7am–10pm, Sun 7am–8pm, Jan–Mar daily 7am–7pm; $10 one-way, $17 round trip). Private service to 15 landings in Boston Harbor.

Rowes Wharf Water Transport (tel: 617-406-8584; www.roweswharfwatertransport.com; Nov–Apr daily 7am–7pm, April–Nov until 10pm; $10 one-way, $17 round trip). Private service to 30 locations in the harbor and beyond.

Arrival by Land

By rail: South Station (Atlantic Avenue and Summer Street) is the east coast terminus for Amtrak (tel: 1-800-872-7245, TDD/TTY 1-800-523-6590; www.amtrak.com). Passengers can travel on northbound trains from Washington, DC, New York, and Philadelphia, with connections from all points in the nationwide Amtrak system. In addition, daily trains arrive from Chicago to Boston by way of Cleveland, Buffalo, Rochester, and Albany NY. Prior to arriving at South Station, the train stops at Back Bay Station (145 Dartmouth Street; tel: 617-345-7958), which is convenient for access to Back Bay and the South End.

By bus: Several intercity bus companies serve Boston. The two largest, **Greyhound** (tel: 1-800-231-2222/214-849-8100; www.greyhound.com) and **Peter Pan** (tel: 1-800-343-9999/1-888-751-8800; www.peterpanbus.com), have daily services to almost anywhere in the US. Greyhound offers a North America Discovery Pass for unlimited travel 7, 15, 30 and 60 days, starting in either the US or Canada and allowing travel to any of their destinations. Services to Cape Cod are provided by **Plymouth & Brockton** (tel: 508-746-0378; www.p-b.com). All buses leave from the bus terminal next to South Station.

By car: Free up-to-date traffic information is available from SmartTraveler (www.smartraveler.com) by dialing 617-374-1234 or 511 on your cell.

From the west: the Massachusetts Turnpike (Mass Pike or I-90) toll road is the best route into town from the west. Take Exit 18 Cambridge/Allston for Cambridge and Harvard Square; Exit 22 Prudential Center/Copley Square for Back Bay, Fenway, Kenmore Square, and Boston Common; Exit 24 for Downtown and access to Route 93.

From the south: Routes 95, 24 and 3 all feed into Route 1 which turns into Route 93 North; Exit 20 (South Station/I-90) is best for Downtown; Exit 23 (Government Center) for Waterfront, and Exit 26 (Storrow Drive) is best for Beacon Hill and Back Bay.

From the north: Routes 95, 1 and 93 enter Boston on elevated highway structures; Exit 26 (Storrow Drive) is best for Beacon Hill and Back Bay; Exit 23B-A (Government Center) is best for North End and Downtown; 20B-A (South Station) is best for Waterfront.

Transportation within Boston

Subway: MBTA (tel: 617-222-3200/1-800-392-6100; www.mbta.com; Mon–Sat 5am–1am, Sun 5.40am–1am)

Above from far left: Leonard P. Zakim Bunker Hill Bridge; travelling on the T; Logan Airport.

LinkPass

A cost-effective way for visitors to use the MBTA system is the LinkPass. It allows unlimited use of the subway, buses, and water shuttles, plus Zone 1A of the commuter rail lines, for one ($9) or seven days ($15), or one month ($59). LinkPass cards can be purchased at almost all stations. Monthly LinkPasses are valid only on subways and buses.

operates the oldest subway in the US. Carriages can get crowded during the rush hours, but it is generally efficient and user-friendly. The four main lines – Red, Green, Orange, and Blue – radiate out from Downtown where the lines intersect; riders can transfer between the lines at no charge. Two Silver Line routes are shown on subway maps, but these are both bus services and charge bus rather than subway fares.

If you need transfer to a bus (also run by the MBTA) you can ask for a transfer at the ticket booth. 'Inbound' means toward Downtown – Park Street, Downtown Crossing, State Street, and Government Center. 'Outbound' means away from Downtown. All four lines have branches that extend beyond central Boston. Check the destination on the front of the trains. Last trains leave Downtown around 12.45am; there are minor differences in the last trains between the lines, so check postings in the station.

To use the subway purchase a Charlie Ticket ($2) from a station machine. A single ticket permits travel on the entire 'Outbound' length of a line, but there is an 'Inbound' surcharge on extensions of the Green Line. If you board the T at surface stations where there is no ticket machine, you will need the exact fare, as conductors do not carry change. The **Charlie Card** (www.mbta.com/fares_and_passes/charlie) is a plastic stored-value card. If you use this then each ride is $1.70, and you can get free transfers to MBTA buses (not possible with the Charlie Tickets). Accompanied children under 11 travel free.

Buses: Few of MBTA's 160-plus bus routes enter Downtown, and most of these are express services from outlying areas. Route 1 travels along Massachusetts Avenue (from Back Bay) across the Charles River to MIT and on to Harvard Square. Single rides are $1.50 or $1.25 using a Charlie Card. Express buses are $2.80–5. Transfers to the subway are discounted only if you are using a Charlie Card. If you do not have the exact fare you will be given change in the form of a Charlie Ticket.

Commuter Rail: The MCTA Commuter Rail (tel: 1-800-392-6100) extends from downtown Boston to as far as 60 miles (almost 100km) away, serving such tourist destinations as Concord and Salem. Trains to the north and the northwest of Boston depart from North Station (135 Causeway Street), while trains to points south and west leave from South Station (Atlantic Avenue and Summer Street). Most south-side commuter trains also stop at Back Bay Station.

Taxis: Boston has plenty of taxis, although on a rainy day this seems barely credible. There are also taxi lines at most hotels and highly trafficked areas. Note that Boston taxis are not allowed to pick up in Cambridge and vice versa. All tolls are paid for by the passenger, and there is no charge for extra passengers, but the driver may add a charge for heavy suitcases. For trips over 12 miles (20km) from Downtown there are flat rates.

The following taxi companies take phone bookings:

Above from far left: Boston skyline at night; trolleys are a quick way of getting to know the city (see p.26); sailing.

Boston:

Boston Cab, tel: 617-536-5010

Checker Cab, tel: 617-536-7000

Town Taxi, tel: 617-536-5000

Cambridge:

Cambridge Checker Cab, tel: 617-497-1500

Yellow Cab, tel: 617-876-5000

Driving and Car Rental

Drivers must be aged 21 or above to rent, and rates may be higher if you are under 25. Child seats are available for an additional cost and are compulsory for children under five or under 40lbs (18kg). The speed limit on Interstate highways is 55–65mph (88–104kmh); in the city and surrounding communities it is 20–30mph (35–45kmh). Right turns at a red traffic signal are permitted unless there is a NO TURN ON RED sign. On entering a roundabout (rotary), you must yield to vehicles already in it.

All the major car rental companies have outlets at the airport.

Avis, tel: 1-800-331-1212; www.avis.com

Budget, tel: 1-800-527-0700; www.budget.com

Dollar Rent A Car, tel: 1-800-800-3665; www.dollar.com

Enterprise, tel: 1-800-261-7331; www.enterprise.com

Hertz, tel: 1-800-654-3131; www.hertz.com

National, tel: 1-800-227-7368; www.nationalcar.com

Rent-A-Wreck, tel: 1-800-944-7501; www.rentawreck.com

Thrifty, tel: 1-800-847-4389: www.thrifty.com

Bicycle Rental

Boston has plenty of dedicated trails that are good for both cyclist and in-line skaters (rollerbladers). Bikes may be rented from:

Boston Bike Tours and Rentals, Boston Common near the Visitor Center; tel: 617-308-5902; www.bostonbiketours.com; June–Aug daily 9am–6.30pm, Apr 15–May 30 and Sept–Oct Sat–Sun and holidays 9am–6.30pm.

Community Bicycle Supply, 496 Tremont Street; tel: 617-542-8623; www.communitybicycle.com; Apr–Aug Mon–Fri 10am–7pm, Sat 10am–6pm, Sun noon–5pm, Sept–Mar, Mon–Sat 10am–6pm, Wed and Fri until 7pm.

V

VISAS

Immigration into the US is handed to the US Citizenship and Immigration Service (tel: 1-800-375-5283; www.uscis.gov). Getting into the country can be a bureaucratic process, depending what country you are coming from. You must have a passport valid for at least six months longer than your intended stay. Visas are required for most nationalities, but a few countries (including the UK and Australia) are part of the Visa Waiver Program that allows its citizens enter the country for 90 days or less without obtaining a visa. The rules are continually evolving, so always check USCIS before you embark on your trip (tel: 202-663-1225; www.travel.state.gov/visa/index.html).

Boston Common and Downtown

The Langham
250 Franklin Street; tel: 617-451-1900; http://boston.langhamhotels.com/index.html; T-stop: State; $$$$
This luxurious hotel is based in the historic landmark that was once the Federal Reserve Bank. Rooms are decorated to reflect the building's opulent history, and it has all the amenities you would expect. Its Café Fleuri offers a brasserie-style menu, and is best-known for its Saturday chocolate bar buffet and elaborate Sunday jazz brunch.

Nine Zero
90 Tremont Street; tel: 617-772-5800; www.ninezero.com; T-stop: Park Street; $$$$
One of Boston's sleekest boutique hotels, offering high-tech, high-speed, high-touch amenities along with personalized service, custom-designed beds and down comforters. The restaurant serves some of the best steaks in town.

The North End and Charlestown

Boston Backpackers Hostel
234 Friend Street; tel: 617-723-0800; www.bostonbackpackers.com; T-stop: North Station or Haymarket; $
Withing walking distance of Beacon Hill, Downtown, and North End, this hostel offers 48 bunkbeds in 10 dormitory rooms. The 19th-century building with a pub downstairs is appealing. Linens are included in the rates, and there is no curfew.

Bulfinch Hotel
107 Merrimac Street; tel: 617-624-0202; www.bulfinchhotel.com; T-stop: North Station or Haymarket; $$$$
Occupying a restored nine-story triangular corner, or flatiron, building, this sophisticated hotel has 80 contemporary-styled, non-smoking rooms and a groovy tapas bar on site.

The Constitution Inn
150 Third Avenue, Charlestown; tel: 617-241-8400/1-800-495-9622; www.constitutioninn.org; T-stop: Haymarket then bus 93; $$
This former YMCA, located near the USS *Constitution*, offers plainly furnished non-smoking rooms, some with kitchenettes. Rates include access to a state-of-the-art health club with an indoor heated pool, sauna, and weight room.

Onyx Hotel
155 Portland Street; tel: 617-557-9955; www.onyxhotel.com; T-stop: Haymarket; $$$
The 112 rooms in this boutique hotel are decorated in a sophisticated palette of black, taupe, and red, and offer all the latest high-tech amenities. Their sleek Ruby Room bar hops at cocktail hour. Pet-friendly.

Price for a double room for one night without breakfast:	
$$$$	over $300
$$$	$200–300
$$	$100–200
$	below $100

Harvard

Charles Hotel

1 Bennett Street, Cambridge;
tel: 617-864-1200; www.charles
hotel.com; T-stop: Harvard; $$$$
The Charles Hotel offers restrained
Shaker-inspired luxury, with incredible
antique quilts gracing the walls,
and impeccable service. All 299
rooms are well appointed and include
high-tech amenities. The Regatta
Bar is a great jazz venue, and the
Rialto restaurant is a mainstay of the
city's gourmet circuit.

Courtyard Boston Cambridge

777 Memorial Drive, Cambridge;
tel: 617-492-777; www.marriott.
com/hotels/travel/boscy-courtyard-
boston-cambridge; T-stop: Central,
then bus 47; $$
Conveniently situated on the Cambridge
side of the Charles River,
equidistant from Harvard and MIT,
this Marriot-run hotel's river-facing
rooms provide the best-value Boston
skyline views.

The Inn at Harvard

1201 Massachusetts Avenue,
Cambridge; tel: 617-491-2222/1-
800-528-0444; www.innat
harvard.com; T-stop: Harvard; $$
Architect and Harvard grad Graham
Gund designed this four-story hotel,
modeled after the Isabella Stewart
Gardner Museum, to blend in with
the university buildings. The 111
rooms built around a four-story
atrium are delightful and were all
recently renovated.

Mary Prentiss Inn

6 Prentiss Street, Cambridge;
tel: 617-661-2929; www.mary
prentissinn.com; T-stop: Porter; $$$
This historic neoclassical Greek Revival
building has 20 rooms with
exposed beams, shutters, and antiques;
some have wood-burning fireplaces
and Jacuzzis. Rates include a full
breakfast and complimentary afternoon
tea. There is a lush outdoor deck,
and free parking.

Charles River and MIT

Kendall Hotel

350 Main Street, Cambridge;
tel: 617-577-1300; www.kendall
hotel.com; T-stop: Kendall/MIT; $$$$
A boutique hotel in a beautifully
renovated 1893 Victorian firehouse,
with 65 antiques-filled rooms; those
in the seven-story tower have Jacuzzi
baths with separate showers. It is
located in the heart of Kendall Square
next to MIT.

Le Meridien Cambridge

20 Sidney Street, Cambridge;
tel: 617-577-0200; www.hotelatmit.
com; T-stop: Central; $$$
As you would expect at a hotel owned
by MIT (but managed by Starwood),
the rooms here are big on gadgets, with
Sony Playstations, dataports, and
ergonomically designed furniture. The
art is from the MIT collection and the
DeCordova Museum in Lincoln *(see
p.87)*. There is a peaceful rooftop
garden, and the hotel is convenient for
Central Square's restaurant and nightlife
scene.

**Above from far
left:** Liberty Hotel,
based in the former
Charles Street Jail
(see p.110).

B&Bs

Bed and breakfast
accommodations
are not thick on the
ground in Boston,
but those that are
can be of a high
standard. A couple
of agencies to try
are Bed & Breakfast
Agency of Boston
(tel: 617-720-3540
or 800-248-9262;
www.boston-bnb
agency.com) and
Bed and Breakfast
Associates Bay
Colony (tel: 888-
486-6018; www.bnb
boston.com). Prices
typically range from
$100 to $160 for a
double room.

Royal Sonesta

5 Cambridge Parkway, Cambridge; tel: 617-806-4200; www.sonesta. com/Boston; T-stop: Lechmere; $$$

Many of the Sonesta's 400 rooms offer great views across the Charles River. There are plenty of facilities, and the hotel is close to the Science Museum, CambridgeSide Galleria, and Kendall Square. Its restaurant Dante serves award-winning Italian fare.

Beacon Hill

Beacon Hill Hotel

25 Charles Street; tel: 617-723-7575; www.beaconhillhotel.com; T-stop: Charles/MGH; $$$

Just steps from Boston Common, this small hotel in a converted 1830s townhouse has 12 traditionally furnished rooms, all with flat-screen TVs and abundant amenities. It is also home to the popular Beacon Hill Bistro *(see p.116)*.

Four Seasons Hotel Boston

200 Boylston Street; tel: 617-338-4400; www.fourseasons.com; T-stop: Arlington; $$$$

Elegance and sybaritic living are the hallmarks of this 15-story, 274-room red-brick hotel overlooking the Public Garden. The service and cuisine, par-ticularly in the restaurant Aujourd'hui, sets standards city wide. High tea in the Bristol Lounge is recommended.

John Jeffries House

14 David G. Mugar Way; tel: 617-367-1866; www.johnjeffrieshouse. com; T-stop: Charles/MGH; $$

This elegant, comfortable 46-room inn offers accommodations ranging from studios to deluxe units for up to three people, most with kitchenettes. Popular with visiting academics to the nearby Massachusetts General Hospital.

Liberty Hotel

215 Charles Street; tel: 617-224-4000; www.libertyhotel.com; T-stop: Charles/MGH; $$$$

The former Charles Street Jail (built in 1851) has been inventively renovated so that each of the 300 rooms integrate the building's history with a crisp, modern aesthetic. Original prison cat-walks linking public spaces and magnificent soaring windows have been preserved. The in-house restaur-ant Clink, stylish bar Alibi, and a new small-plate café are all run by celebrity chef Barbara Lynch.

XV Beacon

15 Beacon Street; tel: 617-670-1500; www.xvbeacon.com; T-stop: Park St; $$$$

One of Boston's first boutique hotels, XV Beacon combines classic opulence, high-tech toys, and high design. All 60 rooms in the 1903 beaux arts building have gas fireplaces, 4-poster beds, CD players, and heated towel racks.

Price for a double room for one night without breakfast:	
$$$$	over $300
$$$	$200–300
$$	$100–200
$	below $100

Back Bay

463 Beacon Street Guest House

463 Beacon Street; tel: 617-536-1302; www.463beacon.com; T-stop: Hynes; $$

This turn-of-the-20th-century brownstone has 20 comfortable and affordable rooms with private baths, phones, and TVs. Many have kitchenettes. It also offers furnished apartments if you need more room or want a longer stay.

Colonnade Hotel

120 Huntington Avenue; tel: 617-424-7000; www.colonnadehotel.com; T-stop: Copley; $$$$

A $20 million renovation completed in 2007 has seen this hotel go sleek and modern. The rooms have a distinct European feel with blonde woods, chrome, and earth tones. Their rooftop pool, 11 stories above the city, is a favorite summer hangout.

The Eliot Suite Hotel

370 Commonwealth Avenue; tel: 617-267-1607; www.eliothotel.com; T-stop: Hynes; $$$

European-style boutique hotel with 95 elegant rooms and suites (some with kitchenettes and sitting areas), and Clio, one of the city's finest restaurants.

Jurys Boston Hotel

350 Stuart Street, Back Bay; tel: 617-266 7200; http://boston hotels.jurysdoyle.com/jurys_boston; T-stop: Arlington; $$$

Located in the former Boston Police Headquarters, Jurys is a fashionable addition to the city's hotel scene. Luxurious rooms offer complimentary wi-fi, multi-head showers, down-filled comforters, and other luxury amenities.

Newbury Guest House

261 Newbury Street; tel: 617-437-7666/1-800-437-7668; www.newbury guesthouse.com; T-stop: Hynes; $$

Three 1880s single-family Victorian homes were renovated in the 1990s to create this elegant 32-room inn. The rooms retain some of the 19th-century decorative details. There are quieter rooms in the back. Breakfast included.

The Taj Boston

15 Arlington Street; tel: 617-536-5700/800-241-3333; www.tajhotels.com; T-stop: Arlington; $$$

Formerly the original Ritz Carlton, some of the rooms and suites at this elegant hotel overlook the Public Garden. If you are lucky enough to have a real fireplace, you can ring the Fireplace Butler, who will offer you a menu of different woods to burn. The ban on denim in the bar and dining room lives on.

Back Bay Fens

The Beech Tree Inn Bed and Breakfast

83 Longwood Avenue, Brookline; tel: 617-277-1620; www.thebeech treeinn.com; T-stop: Longwood; $$

This B&B is bit of a hike west of the Fenway, in a turn-of-the-century Victorian home. Each of its 10 rooms is furnished with books and a fireplace. Breakfast is included, and there is a pleasant backyard patio.

Above from far left: XV Beacon boutique hotel; Liberty Hotel.

Boston International Youth Hostel

12 Hemenway Street; tel: 617-536-1027; www.bostonhostel.org; T-stop: Hynes; $

Year-round budget accommodations in dorms (single-sex and co-ed) and private double rooms, all with shared baths. Non YH-members are accepted, and rates include breakfast. There are kitchen and laundry facilities.

Hotel Commonwealth

500 Commonwealth Avenue; tel: 617-933-5000; www.hotelcommonwealth.com; T-stop: Kenmore; $$$$

This hotel is a destination for locals as well as visitors. Gourmet Bostonians flock to its restaurant, Eastern Standard, which serves excellent French food alongside what is arguably the best cocktail list in town. Rooms feature free wi-fi and marble bathrooms.

Museum of Fine Arts and Isabella Gardner Museum

Best Western – The Inn at Longwood

342 Longwood Avenue; tel: 617-731-4700; fax: 617-731-4870; www.innatlongwood.com; T-stop: Green Line D Train to Longwood; $

Price for a double room for one night without breakfast:	
$$$$	over $300
$$$	$200–300
$$	$100–200
$	below $100

161 nicely furnished and fully equipped rooms in the heart of Longwood Medical Area and near Back Bay attractions.

YMCA of Greater Boston

316 Huntington Avenue, Fenway; tel: 617-536-7800, fax: 617-267-4653; www.ymcaboston.org; T-stop: Orange Line to Northeastern; $

Men-only accommodations in affordable clean rooms. Guests have full use of athletic facilities that are also used by many Boston residents. Maximum stay is 10 days.

The South End

Berkeley Residence YWCA

40 Berkeley Street; tel: 617-375-2524; www.ywcaboston.org/berkeley; T-stop: Back Bay/South End; $

The 200-room facility has gone co-ed, renting singles, doubles and triples. Rooms are basic, and all share two large bathrooms on each floor. Amenities include a dining room, laundry, and central TV area. Rates include breakfast.

Chandler Inn

26 Chandler Street; tel: 617-482-3450/1-800-842-3450; www.chandlerinn.com; T-stop: Back Bay/South End; $$

All 56 rooms at this small, gay-friendly hotel have desks, satellite TVs, and dataports. Some rooms are quite small, as are the baths, but they are comfortable and stylish. If you want quiet, request a room several floors up from the rowdy ground-floor sports bar.

Clarendon Square Inn

198 West Brookline Street; tel: 617-536-2229; www.clarendonsquare.com; T-stop: Back Bay/South End or Symphony; $$

Beautifully appointed, gay-friendly Victorian B&B offering the amenities of a small luxury hotel and the warmth of a small inn. Rooms have wood-burning fireplaces, dataports, and DVD players. The views of the Boston skyline from the rooftop hot tub are fantastic.

Waterfront and Fort Point Channel

Boston Harbor Hotel

70 Rowes Wharf; tel: 617-439-7000; www.bhh.com; T-stop: Aquarium; $$$$

Board the airport water shuttle at Logan and, seven minutes later, step into one of the city's premier waterside hotels. Each of the 230 rooms has either a harbor or skyline view. Eighteen rooms are designed for the physically disabled. Museum-quality art decorates the public areas, and the Meritage offers superb dining. Oenophiles should inquire about their annual wine festival.

Harborside Inn

185 State Street; tel: 617-723-7500/888-723-7565; www.harborsideinnboston.com; T-stop: Aquarium; $$

Not actually on the water, but still in a convenient location for the Waterfront. The 54 rooms in this renovated warehouse have high ceilings, exposed brick walls, oriental rugs, and hardwood floors. Quieter rooms face away from State Street.

Intercontinental Hotel

510 Atlantic Avenue; tel: 617-747-1000; fax: 617-217-5190; www.intercontinentalboston.com; T-stop: Aquarium/South Station; $$$$

The newly built Intercontinental Hotel is well situated between Rowes Wharf, the Children's Museum, South Station, and the Financial District, and is an easy subway or water-taxi ride from Logan Airport. Many of its 423 rooms and suites have Waterfront views. Its Miel 'Brasserie Provençale' restaurant serves high-quality French food 24 hours a day.

Seaport Hotel

1 Seaport Lane; tel: 617-385-4000; www.seaporthotel.com; T-stop: Seaport World Trade Center; $$$$

One of the city's newest Waterfront hotels, Seaport has 427 state-of-the-art rooms with hand-crafted cherry furnishings, marble baths, and desks. The luxurious health club includes a 50ft (15m) heated pool and extensive exercise facilities.

The Westin Boston Waterfront

425 Summer Street; tel: 617-532-4600; www.westin.com; T-stop: World Trade Center; $$$

Sink into one of the Westin's trademark Heavenly Beds at this relatively new hotel which is on the edge of the up-and-coming South Boston Seaport area. There are chic new restaurants and bars nearby, as well as the Institute of Contemporary Art.

Above from far left: outside dining area at the Harborside Inn; red-brick Four Seasons (see p.110).

such as JFK's lobster stew and calf's liver with bacon, are still available, spruced up with Shire's contemporary touches. Denim and sneakers are only allowed in the bar area.

Boston Common and Downtown

Chau Chow City Restaurant

81 Essex Street; tel: 617-338-8158; Mon–Sat 11am–12.45am, Sun 11am–midnight; T-stop: Chinatown; $

One of Chinatown's best destinations for dim sum, this glitzy three-story neon palace serves seafood on two floors, dim sum on one floor, and features a menu with hundreds of dishes.

Hong Kong Eatery

79 Harrison Avenue; tel: 617-423-0838; daily 9am–10.30pm; T-stop: Chinatown; $

A taste of Canton in Downtown Boston. Do not be discouraged by the pigs and ducks in the window: this little restaurant, heavily patronized by Chinese, serves excellent food.

Locke-Ober

3 Winter Place; tel: 617-542-1340; www.lockeober.com; Mon–Thur 11.30am–2.30pm, 5.30–10pm, Fri until 11pm, Sat 5.30–11pm; $$$

Celebrity chef Lydia Shire created a stir when she took over this handsome dining room, which had previously banned women from the premises for 97 years. Many traditional favorites,

such as JFK's lobster stew and calf's liver with bacon, are still available, spruced up with Shire's contemporary touches. Denim and sneakers are only allowed in the bar area.

Sakurabana

57 Broad Street; tel: 617-542-4311; www.sakurabanaonline.com; Mon–Thur 11.30am–9.30pm, Fri 11.30am–10pm, Sat 5pm–10pm; T-stop: State; $$

One of the only Japanese restaurants in this area, with perfunctory decor. However, the lines for lunch are testament to its simple, tasty food, with a few inventive twists.

The North End and Charlestown

Bricco Enoteca and Lounge

241 Hanover Street; tel: 617-248-6800; www.bricco.com; Mon–Fri 5pm–2am, Sat–Sun noon–4pm, 5pm–2am; T-stop: Haymarket; $$$$

An upscale boutique Italian restaurant preparing regional treats such as hand-made pasta. The waiters will urge you to order a 'traditional' meal with several courses, so come prepared with an empty stomach and full wallet.

Grezzo

69 Prince Street; tel: 857-362-7288; www.grezzorestaurant.com; Wed–Sun 5pm–close; T-stop: Haymarket; $$$

One of Boston's few vegan fine-dining experiences. Owner/chef Alissa Cohen serves up vegan versions of Italian favorites like ravioli, gnocchi, and

Price guide for a three-course dinner for one, excluding beverages, tax, and tip:

$$$$	$60 and above
$$$	$40–60
$$	$20–40
$	$20 and below

lasagne. To preserve natural enzymes nothing is cooked over 112°F (44°C). For dessert try the raw cacao cake.

Olives

10 City Square; tel: 617-242-1999; www.toddenglish.com; Mon–Fri 5.30–10pm, Sat 5–10.30pm, Sun 5–9pm; T-stop: Community College; $$$$

The original restaurant that put chef Todd English on the culinary map. Creative Italian cuisine and great use of a wood-fired oven to prepare meats and other dishes served with signature sauces like pistachio pesto.

Pomodoro

319 Hanover Street; tel: 617-367-4348; www.pomodoroboston.com; Tue–Fri 3–11pm, Sat 11am–11pm, Sun 10am–11pm; T-stop: Haymarket; $$

A cozy, casual trattoria serving fresh and tasty dishes based on seasonal local ingredients. Consistent winner of food awards, and favorite among critics and locals. Come early to grab one of the eight tables. Cash only.

Harvard

Café Algiers

40 Brattle Street, Cambridge; tel: 617-492-1557; daily 8.30am–10.45pm; T-stop: Harvard; $$

Hang out with Harvard's boho crowd at this atmospherically North African-styled place, serving a reasonably priced menu of well prepared Middle Eastern standards. The falafel has a unique twist and the handmade lamb sausage is seasoned to perfection. Handy for movies at the adjoining repertory theater.

Casablanca

40 Brattle Street, Cambridge; tel: 617-876-0999; Mon–Thur 11.30am–2.30pm, 5.30–10pm, Fri–Sat until 10.30pm, Sun 11am–3pm, 5.30–10pm; T-stop: Harvard; $$$

In the same complex as Café Algiers, this buzzing and reliable place takes its design cues from the famous Bogart movie. Offers a Mediterranean menu with refreshing interpretations of Middle Eastern dishes; tapas available at the bar tables.

Harvest

44 Brattle Street, Cambridge; tel: 617-868-2255; www.harvestcambridge.com; Mon–Thur noon–2.30, 5.30–10pm, Fri–Sat until 11pm, Sun 11.30am–2.30pm, 5.30–10pm; T-stop: Harvard; $$$

As the name suggests, chef Mary Dumont focuses on the region's freshest seasonal ingredients to prepare dishes interpreted from around the world. The atmosphere is relaxed, but has a distinct business-account feel. It offers dining in one of the few garden terraces around Harvard Square.

Rialto

Charles Hotel, 1 Bennett Street, Cambridge; tel: 617-661-5050; www.rialto-restaurant.com; Mon–Fri 5.30–10pm, Sat 5.30–11pm, Sun 5.30–9pm; T-stop: Harvard; $$$$

Perennial favorite of gourmands. Chef Jody Adams helms this recently renovated restaurant specializing in regional Italian cuisine with a focus on seafood. Menu changes region and

Above from far left: seafood is a staple of New England cooking; lunch in the *Cheers* bar in Beacon Hill (84 Beacon Street); upmarket desert; elegant interior of Locke-Ober.

ingredients seasonally. The wine list offers an interesting range from organic and small vineyards.

Tamarind Bay

75 Winthrop Street, Cambridge; tel: 617-491-4552; www.tamarind-bay. com; Mon–Fri noon–2.30pm, 5–10.30pm, Sat–Sun noon–3pm, 5–10.30pm; T-stop: Harvard; $$$

Far from your standard tandoori and curry joint, Tamarind Bay offers authentic, unusual offerings from the various regions of the Indian subcontinent. The environment is dark and a little more sophisticated than usual too.

Blue Room

1 Kendall Square Complex, Cambridge; tel: 617-494-9034; www.the blueroom.net; Sun 11am–2.30pm, 5.30–10pm, Mon–Thur 5.30–10pm, Fri–Sat 5.30–11pm; T-stop: Kendall Square (10-minute walk); $$$

Comfortable and casual restaurant serving contemporary innovative and eclectic food in a cave-like room. The service is informal but impeccable, and the wine list always includes interesting selections that pair beautifully with the menu.

Helmand Restaurant

143 First Street, Cambridge; tel: 617-492-4646; www.helmand restaurantcambridge.com; Sun–Thur 5–10pm, Fri–Sat 5–11pm; T-stop: Lechmere; $$

A favorite among locals. The food is aromatic, and the flavors are exotic in an area where most of the other restaurants are pretty generic chains that cater to the teenage shoppers at the nearby CambridgeSide Galleria mall.

Salts

798 Main Street, Cambridge; tel: 617-876-8444; www.saltsrestaurant. com; Tue–Sat 6–10pm; T-stop: Central Square; $$$$

Small restaurant serving a limited but focused French-inspired American contemporary menu. Their signature duck is cooked to perfection. The cozy, soothingly decorated room makes this a great place for a romantic meal.

Beacon Hill Bistro

25 Charles Street; tel: 617-723-1133; www.beaconhillhotel.com/bistro.html; Mon–Fri 7–10am, 11.30am–3pm, 5.30–11pm, Sat 7.30–10am, 10am–3pm, 5.30–11pm, Sun 7.30–10am, 10am–3pm, 5.30–10pm; T-stop: Charles/MGH; $$$

French food with a New England influence in a long, narrow room lined with leather banquettes and mirrors. The sophisticated atmosphere makes it ideal for intimate conversation. Weekend brunch is popular.

Price guide for a three-course dinner for one, excluding beverages, tax, and tip:

$$$$	$60 and above
$$$	$40–60
$$	$20–40
$	$20 and below

Bin 26 Enoteca

26 Charles Street; tel: 617-723-5939; www.bin26.com; Mon–Thur noon– 10pm, Fri–Sat noon–11pm, Sun 5.30–10pm; T-stop: Charles/MGH; $$

Not so much a wine bar as a temple to wine. Collages of bottle labels are lacquered on the back wall, and 'chandeliers' of upside-down bottles cover the bathroom ceilings. The wine list has over 60 offerings by the glass. Be sure to stop the manager for his advice on pairing the bar's best with the small and savory dishes.

Lala Rokh

97 Mount Vernon Street; tel: 617-720-5511; www.lalarokh.com; Mon–Fri noon–3pm, 5.30–10pm, Sat–Sun 5.30–10pm; T-stop: Charles/MGH; $$

Sophisticated Persian-inspired cuisine, with elements of Indian, Turkish, and Armenian flavors, in a romantically styled townhouse. The combination of ingredients brings the Middle Eastern food to a new level. Vegetarian-friendly.

No. 9 Park

9 Park Street; tel: 617-742-9991; www.theno9group.com; Mon–Fri 5.30–10pm; T-stop: Park Street; $$$$

Recognized as one of Boston's top restaurants, No. 9 Park prepares European country cuisine in a Bulfinch-designed 19th-century mansion overlooking the Common. Prix-fixe tasting menus change daily, and an à la carte menu is available. A simpler café menu is also available in the bar on a first-come-first-served basis.

Back Bay

Davio's

75 Arlington Street; tel: 617-357-4810; www.davios.com; Mon–Tue 11.30am–3pm, 5–10pm, Wed–Fri 11.30am–3pm, 5–11pm, Sat 5–11pm, Sun 5pm–10pm; T-stop: Arlington; $$$

Based in the historic Paine Furniture Building, Davio's is a local favourite. Its staying power is testament to the quality of its service and food, which is straightforward northern Italian fare using the finest of ingredients. At lunch there is also a takeout counter, serving homemade sandwiches, salads, and soups.

Jasper White's Summer Shack

50 Dalton Street; tel: 617-867-9955; www.summershackrestaurant.com; Nov–Mar Mon–Fri 5–11pm, Apr–Oct Sun–Thur 11.30am–10pm, Fri and Sat 11.30am–11pm; bar until 1am; T-stop: Hynes; $$

Although the word 'shack' is a bit of a stretch, few will quibble as they chow down on pan-roasted lobster, steamers, and fresh seafood chowder.

Sonsie

327 Newbury Street; tel: 617-351-2500; www.sonsieboston.com; Mon–Tue 11.30am–2.30pm, 6–11pm, Wed–Fri until midnight, Sat 11.30am–3pm, 6pm–midnight, Sun 11.30am–3pm, 6–11pm; T-stop: Arlington; $$

Indulge in a spot of people-watching from Sonsie's sidewalk tables. Unusual pizza combos, seasonal menus built around a single ingredient and general menu descriptions might seem overly fussy, but the dishes generally work.

Above from far left: Salts prepares dishes with locally sourced produce; peach gnocchi at the Top of the Hub (see p.60); popular local chain; making fresh pasta at No. 9 Park.

Back Bay Fens

Betty's Wok & Noodle Diner

250 Huntington Avenue; tel: 617-424-1950; www.bettyswokand noodle.com; Mon–Thur noon–10pm, Fri–Sat noon–11pm, Sun noon–10pm; T-stop: Symphony; $$

Casual restaurant featuring an unusual fusion of Asian and Latino cuisines. Noodles are paired with a South American-style citrus sauce, and 'Juantons' are filled with spicy Cuban pork filling. Drinks run from sangria to sake.

Eastern Standard

528 Commonwealth Avenue; tel: 617-532-9100; www.easternstandard boston.com; Mon–Thur 7.30–10am, 11.30am–2.30pm, 5–11pm, Fri–Sat until midnight, Sun 10.30am–3pm, 5–11pm; T-stop: Kenmore; $$$

Next to the Commonwealth Hotel, the menu at this Parisian-style bistro features everything from veal schnitzel to beef Wellington via the classic *moules et frites*. The wine list is long and well picked, and the creative cocktail menu is a labor of love. Single diners can pull up a seat at its 46ft-long bar.

The Mission Bar and Grill

724 Huntington Avenue; tel: 617-566-1244; www.themissionbar.com; daily 11am–midnight; T-stop: Brigham Circle; $$

Maybe Britain's 'gastropub' movement has finally arrived in the US. The mission of this bar seems to be beer, with a respectable list of bottled ales and on-tap brews, served in their native glasses. They also get the food right. Potato skins are made with sweet potatoes, and salads are garnished with homemade croutons, not drowned in oil.

Petit Robert Bistro

468 Commonwealth Avenue; tel: 617-375-0699; www.petitrobert bistro.com; daily 11am–11pm; T-stop: Kenmore; $$

Simple French food without fuss or high prices. Chef Jacky Robert's goal is to create a bistro where diners can eat for under $20. The menu mostly hits this mark, with ingredients from the best purveyors to create upmarket steak frites, lobster bouillabaisse, and croque monsieur. There is a second branch in the South End at 480 Columbus Avenue (tel: 617-867-0600).

Z Square

580 Commonwealth Avenue; tel: 617-425-0101; www.z-square.com; Mon–Thur 7am–10pm, Fri 7am–11pm, Sat 8am–11pm, Sun 8am–10pm; T-stop: Kenmore Square; $$

Imagine an upscale organic supermarket with table service. That is what this California restaurant offers, with its modern, healthy dishes in a simple room flooded with natural light and students. During the day the menu

Price guide for a three-course dinner for one, excluding beverages, tax, and tip:	
$$$$	$60 and above
$$$	$40–60
$$	$20–40
$	$20 and below

focuses on café fare, turning into a full service restaurant in the evening. There is a second location near Harvard Square at 14 J.F. Kennedy Street, Cambridge (tel: 617-576-0101).

The South End

The Butcher Shop

552 Tremont Street; tel: 617-423-4800; www.theno9group.com; Sun–Mon 11am–10pm, Tue–Sat 11am–11pm; T-stop: Back Bay; $$$

One of Boston's top chefs, Barbara Lynch, runs this small wine bar and charcuterie. Stop in for a generous pour of Pinot Noir to accompany a small plate of antipasti, before you nip across the road for a performance at the Boston Center for the Arts.

Delux Café

100 Chandler Street; tel: 617-338-5258; Mon–Sat 5pm–11.30pm; T-stop: Back Bay; $$

The quirky decor of old Elvis records on the walls and Cartoon Network on the television screens make Delux a magnet for hipsters. You cannot go wrong with their famous quesadillas or one of their comfort-food specials.

The Franklin Café

278 Shawmut Avenue; tel: 617-350-0010; www.franklincafe.com; Mon–Sun 5.30–1.30am; T-stop: Back Bay; $$

Delicious bistro-style dishes served in a romantic, darkly lit small space, tucked away on sleepy Shawmut Avenue. Try the seasonal sides, classic cocktails, and daily gourmet specials.

Pho Republique

1415 Washington Street; tel: 617-262-0005; www.phorepublique.net; Mon–Sun 5.30pm–1am; T-stop: Back Bay; $$

Chef Arnond Sreesuvan cooked across Asia before coming to America, and his appealing, creative menu at Pho reflects that journey. The slightly kitsch setting and buzzy vibe make this a late-night hotspot for area hipsters.

Waterfront and Fort Point Channel

No-Name

15 Fish Pier (just off Northern Avenue); 617-338-7539; Mon–Sat 11am–10pm, Sun 11am–9pm; T-stop: World Trade Center; $

The antithesis of a tourist trap, No-Name serves no-frills seafood for reasonable prices in a large dining room simply decorated with blown-up photos of Boston's past. Preparations are simple, but the chowder has a reputation.

Persephone (at The Achilles Project)

283 Summer Street; tel: 617-695-2257; www.achilles-project.com; Mon–Sat 5.30–10pm; T-stop: South Station; $$

By day the Achilles Project is an upscale, edgy boutique, with hot-off-the-runway clothes stored in hanging cubes; at night the cubes are pushed off to the side to reveal Persephone, a modern bar and restaurant. Take a seat at one of the communal tables to try chef Michael Leviton's sustainably sourced small-plate concoctions du jour.

Above from far left: wash it down with Sam Adams; Persephone at The Achilles Project; simple plates of seafood at No-Name.

Bars, Pubs, and Lounges

21st Amendment

150 Bowdoin Street; tel: 617-227-7100; www.21stboston.com; daily; T-stop: Park Street

The 21st Amendment repealed Prohibition, and the lawyers, law students, legislators, and Beacon Hill locals congregating in this cozy dark pub with pews still enjoy that right.

28 Degrees

1 Appleton Street; 617-728-0728; www.28degrees-boston.com; daily; T-stop: Arlington

Named after the optimum chilling temperature for Martinis, this chic bar and restaurant offers soft lighting, comfortable banquettes, and a stylish clientele.

33 Restaurant and Lounge

33 Stanhope Street; tel: 617-572-3311; www.33restaurant.com; Tue–Sat; T-stop: Back Bay

Sleek glam bar and restaurant catering to hipsters and gourmands alike. Downstairs a DJ entertains celebs and VIPs. Anything beyond a drink at the bar requires a reservation.

Alibi

Liberty Hotel, 215 Charles Street; tel: 617-224-4000; www.libertyhotel.com; daily; T-stop: Charles/MGH

Housed in a former jail, this lounge bar fittingly serves drinks in the clink's former drunk tank with blown-up mugshots of Frank Sinatra and Lindsay Lohan leering at patrons, and a cocktail menu listing drinks like 'Doing Thyme.'

The Beehive

541 Tremont Street; tel: 617-423-0069; www.beehiveboston.com; daily; T-stop: Back Bay

Lounge bar of the moment with inventive interior design, stylish crowd, velvet ropes, and a long line on weekends.

Crossroads Irish Pub

495 Beacon Street; tel: 617-262-7371; www.crossroadspubboston.com; T-stop: Hynes

An Irish pub favored by the tenants of the local frat houses. Laid-back atmosphere, large TV screens broadcasting sports games, and dartboards upstairs.

Enormous Room

569 Massachusetts Avenue, Cambridge; tel: 617-491-5550; www.enormous.tv; daily; T-stop: Central

What this far-from-large room lacks in size it makes up for in street cred. An inconspicuous glass door painted with red elephants leads to an appealing lounge packed with groovers.

Felt

533 Washington Street; tel: 617-350-5555; www.feltclubboston.com; Tue–Sat; T-stop: Boylston

Local celebs, such as Ben Affleck and Matt Damon, drop by this happening spot, which combines bar, billiard hall, restaurant, and DJs on Fridays and Saturdays. They have a dress code.

Goody Glover's

50 Salem Street; tel: 617-367-6444; www.goodyglovers.com; daily; T-stop: Haymarket

Above: stylish drinking at 28 Degrees.

Neighborhood landmark named after Irish widow Goodwife Ann Glover, the last Bostonian hanged in 1688 for practicing witchcraft. Traditional Irish grub and laid-back vibe.

Grendel's Den

89 Winthrop Street, Cambridge; tel: 617-491-1160; www.grendelsden.com; daily; T-stop: Harvard

Unpretentious student hangout that gained notoriety in 1982 when it won a historic court case enabling them to use their liquor license within 10 feet of a church.

Jacob Wirth

31 Stuart Street; tel: 617-338-8586; www.jacobwirth.com; daily; T-stop: Boylston Street

Time-warp pub and restaurant in the Theater District, established in 1868, serving an impressive list of beers to accompany the wurst and sauerkraut.

J.J. Foley's Cafe

117 East Berkeley Street; tel: 617-728-9101; daily; T-stop: Arlington

One of a few family-run old-school taverns surviving the South End gentrification wave. In business since 1909, including a Prohibition-era stint as a suspiciously popular shoe store, Foley's is favored by off-duty cops, newspapermen, and nearby factory workers for cheap pints and simple grub.

Les Zygomates Bistro Wine Bar

129 South Street; tel: 617-542-5108; www.winebar.com; Mon–Sat; T-stop: South Station

This atmospheric French bistro offers 40 wines by the glass. Tuesday nights feature wine-tastings with food for $30.

Lucky's Lounge

355 Congress Street; tel: 617-357-5825; www.luckyslounge.com; daily; T-stop: South Station

Old Blue Eyes' spirit lives on at Lucky's, where cool pervades in a warehouse lounge with old photographs and outstanding Martinis that recall Rat Pack hip.

Kitty O'Shea's

131 State Street; tel: 617-725-0100; www.kittyosheasboston.com; daily; T-stop: State Street

American outpost of the Irish original, housed in a historic stone building with the expected cod Victoriana fixtures and artifacts.

Match

94 Massachusetts Avenue; tel: 617-247-9922; www.matchbackbay.com; daily; T-stop: Hynes

Martinis are matched with burgers in this quasi-bachelor pad, with a chill-out throbbing soundtrack.

Middlesex

315 Massachusetts Avenue, Cambridge: tel: 617-868-6739; www.middlesexlounge.com; daily; T-stop: Central

At around 10pm the low, sleek furniture is rolled to the edges of the room, and the space becomes a dance floor packed with a hip, cosmopolitan crowd. Go before 11pm to skip the legendary line.

Opening Hours
Bars, pubs, and lounges typically open around 4 or 5pm. By law they all have to stop serving alcohol at 2am (1am Sunday to Wednesday in Cambridge).

Comedy Scene
Among the top US comedians to have kick-started their careers in Boston are Denis Leary and Conan O'Brien. A couple of places that have both being going for 25 years are ImprovBoston (40 Prospect Street, Cambridge; tel: 617-576-1253; www.improvboston.com; Wed–Sat 8pm, Sun 7pm; T-stop: Central; charge) and Comedy Connection (Faneuil Hall, 2nd floor, Quincy Market Building; tel: 617-248-9700; www.symfonee.com/comedyconnection/boston; T-stop: Government Center; charge).

River Gods
125 River Street, Cambridge; tel: 617-576-1881; www.rivergods online.com; daily; T-stop: Central
Neighborhood pub with a quirky sense of style. Local artwork, furniture that looks as though it was randomly picked from several second-hand shops, and alternative rock all add to its charm.

Sevens Ale House
77 Charles Street; tel: 617-523-9074; www.sevensalehouse.com; daily; T-stop: Charles/MGH
Refreshingly down to earth for ritzy Beacon Hill, this small rustic pub gets pretty rowdy on game nights. A game of darts can become a dangerous sport on packed weekend nights.

Live Music

Berklee College of Music
1140 Boylston Street, Cambridge; tel: 617-266-1400; www.berklee.edu; T-stop: Hynes; charge
Founded in 1945, this is the world's largest independent music college, with a highly regarded jazz program that attracts students from around the globe. Past alumni include Quincy Jones, Melissa Etheridge, Donald Fagen, and Branford Marsalis. Faculty, student, and recording artists regularly perform in one of the college's many venues.

Club Passim
47 Palmer Street; tel: 617-492-7679; www.clubpassim.org; T-stop: Harvard; charge
The US's oldest folk club, Passim hosts a variety of local and national artists, focusing on folk, world, and bluegrass music.

The Middle East Club
472 Massachusetts Avenue, Cambridge; tel: 617-864-3278; www.mideastclub.com; T-stop: Central; charge
A variety of acts play in this complex's various rooms, where the walls are adorned with local artists' work.

Paradise Rock Club
967–969 Commonwealth Avenue; tel: 617-562-8800; www.thedise.com; daily 6pm–2am; T-stop Pleasant Street; charge
Boston's top venue for established and up-and-coming rock and alt. pop music talents. For over a quarter of a century it has hosted everyone from U2 and The Police to Bloc Party and the Fratellis.

Regatta Bar
Charles Hotel, 1 Bennett Street, Cambridge; tel: 617-661-5000; www.regattabarjazz.com; T-stop: Harvard; charge
Fashionable bar featuring well-known jazz and R&B acts in a sophisticated interior. Bookings recommended.

Toad
1912 Massachusetts Avenue, Cambridge; tel: 617-497-4950; www.toadcambridge.com; Mon–Wed 5pm–1am, Thur–Sat 5pm–2am, Sun 6pm–1am; T-stop: Porter Square
Bands perform live every night at this cozy neighborhood bar (room for just 62 customers) with no cover charge. Pearl Jam have done impromptu gigs here when they are in town.

T.T. the Bear's Place

10 Brookline Street, Cambridge; tel: 617-492-0082; www.ttthebears. com; daily; T-stop: Central; charge

One of the best places in greater Boston to catch live music, in a relaxed, friendly atmosphere. Last-minute tickets can be bought at the door with cash only.

Wally's Café

427 Massachusetts Avenue; tel: 617-424-1408; www.wallys cafe.com; daily; T-stop; Massachusetts Avenue

Hole-in-the-wall bar with jamming locals performing nightly. Named after founder Joseph L. Walcott, who opened the original bar across the street in 1947.

Above from far left: studenty Grendel's Den (see p.121); folk music at Club Passim.

Gay Scene

The Alley

Pl Alley, 275 Washington Street; tel: 617-263-1449; www.thealley bar.com; daily; T-stop: Park Street

Flying the flag for the Downtown gay community, this casual, friendly pub is the home of the annual Bearapalooza for the hirsute and their admirers.

Club Café

209 Columbus Avenue; tel: 617-536-0966; www.clubcafe.com; daily; T-stop: Arlington

Popular gay complex, and place to be on Thursday nights; quieter bar and restaurant at the front.

Machine

1256 Boylston Street; tel: 617-536-1950; www.nightclubmachine.com; daily; T-stop: Kenmore; charge

Grab your leather and chains for this grungy nightclub with pool hall and a leather bar upstairs. Its busiest night is Friday.

Dance Clubs

Aria

Wilbur Theatre, 246 Tremont Street; tel: 617-338-7080; www.ariaboston. com; Thur–Sat; T-stop: Boylston; charge

A slightly more mature crowd congregates at this sleek cocktail lounge and nightclub, with velvet couches and intimate dance floor.

Mojitos

48 Winter Street; tel: 617-988-8123; www.mojitoslounge.com; Thur–Sun 9pm–2am; T-stop: Boylston; charge

Multi-level club for those who move to a Latin beat or want to learn (lessons kick off at 9.15pm).

The Roxy

Roxyplex, 279 Tremont Street; tel: 617-338-7699; www.roxyboston. com; Fri–Sat; T-stop: Boylston; charge

One of Boston's largest clubs, with seven bars, balconies, and a huge dance floor that also hosts live performances. Friday night is techno music, and Saturday is gay night.

Rumor

100 Warrenton Street; tel: 617-422-0045; www.rumorboston.com; Tue–Sun; T-stop: Boylston; charge

Considered by many to be Boston's best club. Wednesday's gay night is very popular with all sexual persuasions.

Clubbing Rules

For dance clubs you will typically pay an entrance fee of between $10 and $20, depending on the night and the DJ playing. Strict liquor-licencing laws means all clubs shut at 2am, with the sole exception of the members-only club Rise (306 Stuart Street; tel: 671-423-7473; www.riseclub.us). Many places also enforce a dress code prohibiting sportswear, sneakers, and baseball caps. Check websites or call for details before heading out.

CREDITS

Insight Step by Step Boston
Written by: Simon Richmond
Edited by: Alex Knights
Series Editor: Clare Peel
Cartography Editors: Zoë Goodwin
and James Macdonald
Picture Manager: Steven Lawrence
Art Editor: Ian Spick
Production: Kenneth Chan
Photography by: Apa: Richard, Daniela, and
Abraham Nowitz (also Marcus Brooke, Mark
Read, and Carlotta Junger), except: istock photo
8TL, 12TM, 26TL, 44TM, 76–7T, 84TL, 89TR,
90TL, 92TL, 92–3T, 94–5T; Jon Arnold 68–9T;
Mary Evans 21; Peter Newark's American Pictures
20; Rex Features 68TL; courtesy of the Museum of
Fine Arts, Boston 65TR, 65BL.
Cover: main image: Atlantide Phototravel/Corbis;
bottom left and right: Abraham Nowitz/APA.
Printed by: Insight Print Services (Pte) Ltd,
38 Joo Koon Road, Singapore 628990

www.insightguides.com

DISTRIBUTION

Worldwide
**Apa Publications GmbH & Co. Verlag KG
(Singapore branch)**, 38 Joo Koon Road,
Singapore 628990
Tel: (65) 6865 1600
Fax: (65) 6861 6438

UK and Ireland
GeoCenter International Ltd
Meridian House, Churchill Way West,
Basingstoke, Hampshire, RG21 6YR
Tel: (44) 01256 817 987
Fax: (44) 01256 817 988

United States
Langenscheidt Publishers, Inc.
36–36 33rd Street, 4th Floor,
Long Island City, NY 11106
Tel: (1) 718 784 0055
Fax: (1) 718 784 0640

Australia
Universal Publishers
1 Waterloo Road, Macquarie Park, NSW 2113
Tel: (61) 2 9857 3700
Fax: (61) 2 9888 9074

New Zealand
Hema Maps New Zealand Ltd (HNZ)
Unit D, 24 Ra ORA Drive,
East Tamaki, Auckland
Tel: (64) 9 273 6459
Fax: (64) 9 273 6479

CONTACTING THE EDITORS

We would appreciate it if readers would alert us
to errors or outdated information by writing to
us at insight@apaguide.co.uk or Apa Publications,
PO Box 7910, London SE1 1WE, UK.

INDEX